Narrow Gauge Railways

Wales and the Western Front

NARROW GAUGE RAILWAYS

WALES AND THE WESTERN FRONT

HUMPHREY HOUSEHOLD

First published by Alan Sutton Publishing 1988

Copyright © Humphrey Household 1988

This edition published 1996 by The Promotional Reprint Company Ltd,
Kiln House, 210 New Kings Road, London SW6 4NZ
exclusively for Bookmart Limited, Desford Road, Enderby,
Leicester LE9 5AD

ISBN 185648 344 4

Printed and bound in China

To
STEWART
who shares my interest
ANGELA
kind hostess who bears railway matters resignedly
and their two young sons
MARCUS magnus
and
MATTHEW

CONTENTS

INTRODUCTION

Narrow gauge railways fascinate many people by their unique character, for each one is different. In the past, some of them were inclined to be wayward, and on the whole their charms were therefore less likely to appeal to those who depended on their services than to the occasional visitor!

I will not go so far as to say that they interested me more than did the main line railways, but they intrigued me, and I have seldom missed an opportunity to see, and if possible travel on, any within reach. In general, staff tolerated visitors who showed genuine interest and were ready to answer questions about equipment and operation put by those with some understanding of railway matters. Undoubtedly one of their special attractions was, that with speeds kept low, they could afford to be less strict about trespass, and indeed staff often encouraged photography in areas from which the public was excluded.

The happy hunting ground has, of course, always been Wales, and I was fortunate in being able to visit five of the railways in the Principality in 1925 while they still served their communities as general carriers of passengers and freight. Only two of those five remain operational today, and it has been delightful to see them again recently and find them in good health, although now solely dependent on the tourist trade. Besides the Welsh lines I did, of course, see others during the years 1924–1935 in Cumberland, Devon, Dorset and Yorkshire, not all of which catered for passenger traffic, and much later, one in Kent.

If this book has any merit, it is that of personal observation and information gathered fifty or more years ago. But of necessity the story of the railways looks back to their origins and on to the later years as chronicled in the technical and daily press, for I have always followed news of their demise, revival or progress with great interest, whether tinged with sorrow or satisfaction. Historically, my chapters depend on the work of others, except in the case of the Corris Railway whose story is almost entirely based on original research into the collection preserved in the Public Record Office at Kew. The inclusion of a chapter on the War Department Light Railways extensively used on the Western Front during the 1914–18 war, although I never saw them, has been prompted by the post-war acquisition of surplus material by a number of British narrow gauge railways, several of which were Welsh, although the largest user was the Ashover Light Railway in Derbyshire. The complete story of those WD lines and their vitally important contribution to the war effort is a very interesting one, fully covered in W.J.K. Davies's book, *Light Railways of the First World War*, on which my chapter is based.

I am indebted to the *Railway Magazine* for permission to use their maps of the Corris and neighbouring lines and the Ashover Light Railway; to J.B. Snell for Festiniog photographs; Lens of Sutton for supplying photographs of the WD railways; the Public Record Office for details of their Corris material and for access to it; the Welsh Highland Railway Society; the Corris Railway Society; the Historical Model Railway Society; the Oakwood Press; and to many of those associated with the Festiniog and Talyllyn Railways who have helped me in conversation or correspondence. I hasten to add that none of these sources is to blame for any errors that may remain.

Once again, I thank the staff of Ashford Public Library for the unfailing help and courtesy they have shown me, and for their patience in responding to my frequent requests to extend the period for books borrowed from their remarkable Railway Room. Housing over 5,500 titles, this Railway Room is believed to hold the largest collection of its kind in the country to which the public has ready access. Finally, I thank the Guildhall Camera Centre in Folkestone for the trouble they have taken to produce good prints for me, often no easy task when working from my own negatives or from faded old postcards.

The source of all photographs reproduced has been acknowledged individually in the captions, except in the case of my own.

Humphrey Household
Folkestone, August 1987

CHAPTER ONE

THE FESTINIOG POINTS THE WAY

Throughout the seventeenth and eighteenth centuries wagonways spread in the coalfields of the midlands and north-east. Most of these made their way from mines in hilly areas to seaports or riverside wharves, descending by a gentle gradient so that laden wagons could run downhill by gravity and the empties be drawn up by a horse. The descent might be divided into stages, each horse toiling up one stage and then riding down in a dandy-cart attached to the rear of a rake of wagons. As the dandy-cart was fitted with a manger, the horse soon learnt to board it of his own accord and feed as he rode. Where the descent was sudden and steep, laden wagons were lowered down a rope-worked incline, drawing up empties as they did so. In the north-east, the rails were laid to a gauge approximating to the standard of today, 4ft. 8½in.

In North Wales, however, the minerals often had to be quarried high up on mountainsides accessible only along narrow valleys whose floors dropped steeply before reaching any point of shipment. The drop from the quarry itself could be overcome by an incline, but the gradual descent of the valley might involve formation of a ledge on the mountain side, the cost of which could be reduced considerably by using a narrower gauge traversing sharp curves. During the first quarter of the nineteenth century, several such lines were built to serve slate quarries using a gauge of about two feet.★

Meantime, the steam locomotive developed rapidly on the railways of the north-east coalfield until it became reliable enough between 1825 and 1830 to carry passengers and freight on public railways. In Wales steam would

★ Often referred to simply as the two-foot gauge, it was generally 1ft. 11½in. in Britain and 60cm. on the Continent.

Sharp curves on a ledge following the contour: Festiniog Railway train between Dduallt and Tan-y-Bwlch, photographed from the last coach on 4 August 1925.

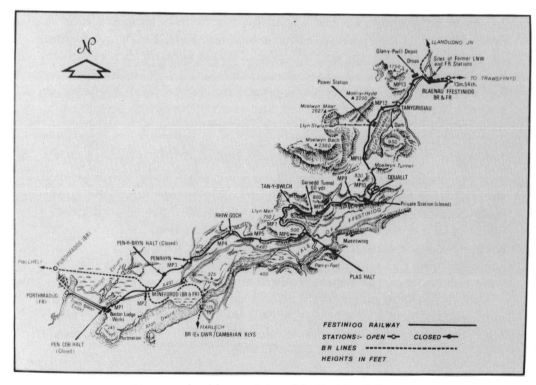

Map, reproduced by permission of the Festiniog Railway.

certainly have been useful to haul trains of returning empties, but some engineers doubted whether it was possible to design and build a locomotive to work effectively along the very narrow gauge tracks in use.

Few among the thousands of tourists who now visit the Festiniog Railway are likely to be aware that this was where the pioneer work was done which not only showed that such a locomotive could be built but also that it was capable of operating an efficient public service. Fewer still will be aware that what was, in the 1860s, an obscure little railway in an unfrequented part of North Wales therefore came to exercise worldwide influence, for it was soon realised that narrow gauge railways with sharper curves and stiffer gradients involved much less expensive engineering features, and so could provide economic transport in countries where the terrain was difficult and traffic likely to be sparse. The gauge did not need to be as narrow as the Festiniog's; something wider would be more suitable for lines likely to develop later into extensive systems.

After the success of the Festiniog engines had been fully and enthusiastically described in the technical press, engineers and railway promoters came from many parts of the world in the late 1860s and 1870s to see for themselves what had been achieved in North Wales. Among them was an American, General W.J. Palmer, a noted railway entrepreneur, who believed the cost of construction on the Stephenson gauge would be a crippling handicap in opening up the Middle West; after visiting the Festiniog he adopted a gauge of 3ft. for his Denver & Rio Grande Railway. In 1870, a Russian Commission watched trials on the Festiniog, together with representatives from France, Germany, Norway and Sweden. Another Commission came from South Africa and, although some lines using the Stephenson gauge had already been built near the coast, in 1873 the members recommended that 3ft. 6in. should be adopted as the country's standard in order to reduce the cost of driving northwards through the mountains. In 1871, a consulting engineer visited the Festiniog on behalf of the Government of India, and although he reported against the introduction of narrow gauges because of the nuisance of transhipment to the 5ft. 6in. gauge main lines, many Indian feeder railways were subsequently built to narrower gauges, including one of the most appealing of all, the Darjeeling–Himalayan Railway, one of the few which adopted the actual Festiniog gauge. Begun in 1879, it is more than fifty miles long and climbs 7,000 ft. into the foothills of the mountains by a series of single and double loops.

In 1870 a gauge of 3ft. 6in. was adopted as standard in both New Zealand and Japan; and in South America a railway across the Andes, begun in 1873, used gauges of 2ft. 6in. and 1m. Metre gauge spread to many areas in the latter part of the nineteenth century, including Burma, Malaya, Siam and

3ft. 6in. gauge, mixed train at Grahamstown, Cape Province. Photographed by my father, H.W. Household, in April 1910.

Grahamstown station, from a card postmarked 19 March 1910, sent by my father who commented that very few trains served it, perhaps three or four a day.

A double spiral on the Darjeeling–Himalayan Railway, begun 1879, 1ft. 11½in. gauge. The train had climbed from the low level seen on the right, circled around behind the building to emerge on the extreme left, and passed under the upper loop on which it stands. From an old postcard.

1 m. gauge. The Kalka Simla Railway, opened 1903, climbed into the hills by winding along rock ledges, through tunnels and over viaducts, gaining height by a series of horseshoe loops one above the other. From an old postcard.

Gauge 3ft. 6in. In the Manawatu Gorge. From an old postcard, pre-1917.

Freight train on the line through the Otira Tunnel, South Island, electrified and opened in 1923. From a set of postcards on sale at the Wembley Exhibition 1924–5.

SWITZERLAND

1m. gauge. The Rhaetian Railway, owned by a private company and now electrified, is an important and extensive metre gauge system in Canton Grisons. The earliest part of it, the Landquart–Klosters–Davos line, was opened 1889–90, and these two views of it in the Davos area are from postcards sent to me by my parents in December 1909 and January 1910.

FRANCE

1m. gauge secondary railways. The station at Orly-sur-Morin, Département Seine et Marne. The Grand Morin and the Petit Morin are tributaries of the River Marne. The neat two-storey station house is adjoined by a goods shed. From a card postmarked 16 August 1908.

C de F des Côtes du Nord, 1m. gauge. Early morning train climbing along the street at Sables d'Or les Pins, Brittany, 27 August 1931. Twenty-five years later the railway was closed.

1 m. gauge C de F Vicinales. The station at Le Coq or Den Haan. As can be seen, in August 1935 the line carried freight as well as passengers.

Train from Ostend approaching Le Coq. In the streets of Ostend it was an urban tramway, but once out of the town it ran on reserved track at a very respectable speed, as seen here on 16 August 1935.

East Africa, whilst in Switzerland it was used for what developed into the mountainous Rhaetian Railway.

In Britain from 1865 onwards, narrow gauge railways operated by steam locomotives were built to serve local needs in other parts of Wales, in Cumberland, Suffolk, Sussex, Devon, Derbyshire, Yorkshire, Scotland, and Ireland. Most of these were formed during the forty years up to 1904, but at least three were promoted and built in the 1920s, no doubt encouraged by the extensive use of 60cm. railways on the Western Front during the 1914–18 war and the locomotives and other material which afterwards became available cheaply from Government disposal boards. Britain, however, never had the like of the widespread local *chemins de fer economiques* and *vicinaux* to be seen in France, Belgium and Holland.

The Festiniog Railway owed its success and its influence to five perspicacious men: William Madocks, James Spooner, Henry Archer, Charles Easton Spooner (James's son), and Robert Fairlie. In 1798, Madocks bought an estate to the north of Traeth Mawr, the estuary of the Afon Glaslyn, and determined to reclaim the marshland and tidal sands. Between 1808 and 1811, he built The Cob, a stone embankment 1600 yards long, to exclude the tide, providing sluices at the northern end for the waters of the Glaslyn to escape. Thus constricted, those waters scoured out a deep channel, action he had not foreseen but which enabled him to create a new harbour, opened in 1824, which he named Port Madoc. He had used iron railways in building the causeway, and he suggested that slate quarrying around Ffestiniog could be greatly developed if a railway were to be built down the Vale of Ffestiniog★ and across The Cob to the new port.

This of course is what the Festiniog Railway eventually did, but the Act for its construction was not obtained until 1832, nearly four years after William Madock's death.

Henry Archer was a principal promoter, and after two attempts to win Parliamentary sanction had failed, he worked hard to ensure the success of the third. Moreover, he saw to the raising of the necessary capital – not in North Wales as might have been expected, but from friends in his native city of Dublin, where indeed the entire original sum was subscribed. The Act named him as Managing Director, and he played an active part in construction until he quarrelled violently with the other directors.

★ Here we encounter the problem of spelling: the Welsh can put two ffs into the name of the town, but not into that of the railway company, whose name was enacted by Parliament in 1832. Porthmadog however seems odd, because the nineteenth-century port had nothing to do with the twelfth-century Welsh Prince Madog, whereas the previous spelling 'Portmadoc' recognised that it was named after its founder, William Madocks.

Of James Spooner little appears to be known before he came to Wales about 1825, apparently on holiday, and became interested in surveying, but he it was who, after one remarkable failure, surveyed the route which eventually won Parliamentary approval. Assisted by Thomas Pritchard, an engineer who had worked under George Stephenson on the Liverpool & Manchester Railway, he produced a masterly plan that ensured maximum economy in operation. Slate from the quarries was brought down self-acting inclines to two branch lines, one from Duffws and the other from Dinas, which united close to the site of the future town of Blaenau Ffestiniog, and from there, once Moelwyn Tunnel had been completed, the line descended uninterruptedly on an average gradient of 1 in 92 for 12¼ miles to The Cob, across which it was almost level to the terminus on the quays of Portmadoc Harbour. To achieve this, the route wound along the contours by sharp curves, made a U-bend around the flanks of a side valley, crossed embankments built up to a height of 60ft. with dry-stone walling, followed ledges cut in rock, and twice threaded tunnels piercing mountain spurs. On a track so aligned, trains of laden wagons were able to descend by gravity all the way from the upper junction at Blaenau Ffestiniog to the near end of The Cob, whence horses drew them to the quayside; and it was within the capacity of horses to haul the returning empties against the grade. The ascent was divided into stages, with a stable at each, so that after working hard against the collar for several miles, the horse was able to rest while riding down in a dandy-cart to the beginning of his stage. Horses were moved about so that each had a share of the harder and easier stages. Gravity-worked Down trains took about 1 hour 40 minutes, but horsedrawn Up trains 5 hours 50 minutes.

James Spooner was not only the engineer who surveyed the route, but also the driving force behind the railway's administration from its opening in 1836 until his death in 1856, first as Clerk to the Company and from 1845 Secretary as well. His successor, appointed Manager and Clerk, was his son, Charles Easton Spooner, who had long been involved in his father's work, for he had left school before he was fifteen to assist in building the line, and had already served ten years as Treasurer. It was he who, during more than thirty years as manager, transformed the horse-worked mineral railway into the miniature main line of worldwide influence. Until then, the only regular travellers had been quarrymen going to and fro between Portmadoc and Blaenau Ffestiniog, but the scenic beauties of the route had already been recognised, and it is believed that a few early visitors had made journeys over it. Clearly, tourist and local passenger traffic could be developed, but only if track and alignment were improved, locomotives introduced, and the carriage of passengers approved by the Board of Trade. Approval, however,

Festiniog Railway Engineering: the U-bend round Llyn Mair. The track descends from the short Garnedd Tunnel to Tan-y-Bwlch station, which stands above the head of the lake, and then returns through the woods on the opposite side of the valley. *(Photograph: J.B. Snell.)*

Typical of James Spooner's engineering: the track on a ledge, rock on the right, a steep drop on the left. *(Photograph: J.B. Snell.)*

One of the early Festiniog Railway 0-4-0 saddle tank locomotives with a tender, *Princess*, built by G. England & Co. in 1863 and seen here *c.* 1923. *(Photograph: Topical Press Agency.)*

might not be easy to obtain: the Gauge Act of 1846 was intended to prevent the spread of passenger carrying railways on other than the standard gauge, but the prohibition was hedged and there were gaps that allowed exceptions.

Meantime, Charles Easton Spooner eased the worst curves by widening cuttings and forming deviations, some of which involved substantial new construction, and relaid the track with much heavier rails more firmly supported. The first engines were delivered in 1863–4, four 0-4-0 tank locomotives of similar design with four-wheeled tenders to carry coal, built by George England & Co., London; their driving wheels were 2ft. in diameter, cylinders 8 × 12in., the boiler pressure was 200lb. (later reduced to 140), and weight 7½ tons. Their performance showed that useful steam locomotives could indeed be designed for such a narrow gauge, and it is a tribute to their builder that one, *Prince*, still exists in working order after 123 years, albeit with many parts renewed.

The railway had been closely inspected on 27 October 1864 on behalf of the Board of Trade by Captain H.W. Tyler, who thought highly of it, and when the recommendations he then made had been attended to, he made a second inspection and gave his approval to the running of passenger trains, for he was well aware that narrow gauge railways could provide economical transport, especially abroad. This was enough, and after passengers had been carried experimentally for some months at their own risk and without payment, the regular passenger service began on 6 January 1865. Trains were at first limited to a speed of 10 mph, but later, Captain Tyler, obviously impressed by the management's responsible attitude, left them free to impose their own limits.

However, neither the four original engines, nor two larger ones built by George England in 1867 with wheels 2ft. 8in. diameter and cylinders 8⅛ × 12in., proved powerful enough for uphill work with passenger coaches and a long tail of empty wagons; and if shorter and more frequent trains were going to be necessary, the track would certainly have to be doubled. As widening rock ledges, tunnels and dry-stone embankments would be vastly expensive, C.E. Spooner sought an alternative. He believed one could be found in the double engines recently designed by Robert Fairlie.

The Fairlie engines had two boilers fitted back to back on one frame mounted on two four-coupled driving bogies, and so had the power and flexibility the Festiniog needed. *Little Wonder*, again built by George England, appeared in 1869, and on test against the earlier locomotives showed that she was capable of handling a greatly increased load against the gradient, that her consumption of fuel was more economical, and that she rode easily round the curves at speeds up to 35 mph. Her success solved the problem of how to increase line capacity – Up journeys, for example, took less than two hours instead of nearly six – and it was her trials that convinced the overseas delegates that narrow gauge railways could be useful in their own countries.

Although Robert Fairlie's design of double bogie engines was not entirely original he managed to patent it, but because of the publicity gained by the tests of *Little Wonder* he exempted the Festiniog from payment of royalties. Three more double engines followed in 1872, 1879 and 1885, with driving wheels 2ft. 8in. or 2ft. 9in. diameter, four cylinders 8½ or 9in. × 14in., pressure 140lb. and weight 20 to 24 tons. They proved so useful and became such a hallmark of the line that, when another locomotive was needed in 1979, a new Fairlie was built and *Earl of Merioneth – Iarll Meirionnydd* joined the hundred-year-old *Merddin Emrys* in present day operation.★

The first carriages were primitive four-wheeled vehicles, box-like with very low floors because roof height was restricted by the dimensions of Moelwyn Tunnel, but from 1871 onwards new coaches were mounted, like the engines, on bogies. This is another indication of the management's

---

★ About three hundred Fairlie double engines were built 'for use throughout the world', according to *The Railway Magazine* July 1986, which commented that the Festiniog examples are, 'so far as is known', the only ones still in working order.

Double boiler Fairlie locomotive *James Spooner* built by the Avonside Engine Co. in 1872, shown at Portmadoc Harbour in 1875. The driver stood on one side of the central firebox and the fireman on the other, both at first unprotected from the weather. *(Photograph: Festiniog Railway.)*

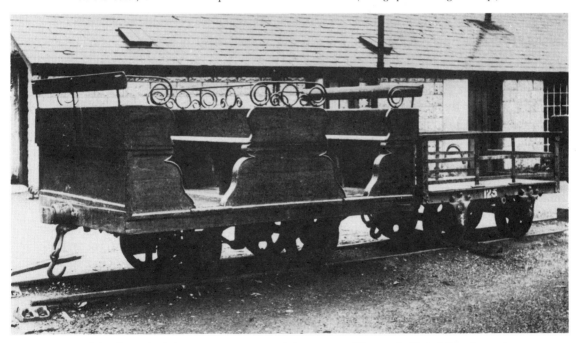

Festiniog four-wheeled open passenger car and slate wagon. *(Photograph: Topical Press Agency.)* The small four-wheeled carriages referred to in the text can be clearly seen in the photograph on page 43 of a train crossing Portmadoc High Street on 4 August 1925; two have open 'observation' sides and a third has glazed windows.

Festiniog Railway bogie coach built by the Gloucester Wagon Co. in 1879, not yet mounted on its bogies and obviously on display at the Gloucester Works. *(Photograph: Historical Model Railway Society, Gloucester Railway Carriage & Wagon Co. collection.)*

enterprise, for they are believed to have been the first bogie coaches in use on the eastern side of the Atlantic Ocean; they were certainly the first in Britain, appearing three years or so before those introduced on the Great Northern and Midland Railways.

As befitted a miniature main line, the Festiniog conformed fully to the Regulation of Railways Act of 1889, and by 1893 block signalling and interlocking of points and signals had been installed, and locomotives and coaches equipped with the vacuum brake. By then steel rails had been laid throughout on main running lines. A further step was the introduction of the electric train staff in 1912. Such careful operation of the traffic was abandoned after a Light Railway Order was obtained at the end of January 1923, granting exemption from statutory signalling regulations. This was implemented during the time when the Festiniog formed part of the light railway 'empire' of Colonel H.F. Stephens, appointed Civil Engineer and Locomotive Superintendent in 1923, and its operation was controlled from his office in Tonbridge, Kent, with stringent economy and little understanding of local problems. Light railway methods were not liked, particularly by the Festiniog enginemen, who insisted on the restoration of protection for single line working.

Tan-y-Bwlch; exchanging the single line train staff – the Miniature Electric Staff system was installed in 1912. Bessie Jones, in Welsh national costume, was stationmistress at Tan-y-Bwlch for many years. *(From a postcard published by the Photochrom Co.)*

Festiniog Railway disc signal near Penrhyndeudraeth *c.* 1923 – this type acted as a distant signal on the approach to a station. *(Photograph: Topical Press Agency.)*

Festiniog Railway double-arm signal post at Tan-y-Bwlch *c.* 1923 – this kind controlled entry to and exit from the station. *(Photograph: Topical Press Agency.)*

Festiniog Railway slate train on a gravity run, passing Ddaullt about 1905. Evidently it was a sight that appealed to the local children, alerted by the noise of its approach, some of whom are seen seated on one of the massive FR slate milestones. *(Photograph: Festiniog Railway.)*

Slate traffic grew to 112,000 tons in 1867, and exceeded 100,000 tons annually for all but eight of the succeeding forty years, rising to a maximum of 139,000 in 1897, enabling the Company to pay dividends of 8 per cent. It was still carried down in long gravity trains of the railway Company's own four-wheeled wagons, snaking their way around the curves, controlled by brakesmen riding the load. As relatively few wagons had any form of brake, the Company's rules laid down that the train must be so marshalled that there was one braked wagon in every five, that speed should not exceed 10 mph, and that 'The greatest caution and vigilance must be observed by the Brakesmen'. Of these men, there were to be not less than two, and if the number of wagons was between 80 and the limit of 120, then there had to be three. The 10 mph limit was not always observed (what speed limits are?) and as 30 to 40 mph could be attained on favourable stretches, a gravity run must have been most exciting to watch; its advent was heralded by three blasts on a sawn-off hunting horn, and as the train passed with a roar of wheels on rails, the men would be seen jumping from wagon to wagon to apply the brakes before reaching the next sharp curve or station. Obviously there were inherent risks in running these trains, for they could not be

Slate wagons built by the GWR at Swindon Works in November 1899, tare weight 17 cwt 2 qr, with a capacity of 2½ tons of slate. The Craigddhu Quarry to the east of Blaenau Ffestiniog connected only with the GWR branch line from Bala Junction and, rather than establish another point of transhipment, the GWR ran the narrow gauge wagons aboard flat wagons fitted with narrow gauge rails and transported them to their exchange sidings with the Festiniog Railway at Blaenau Ffestiniog. Presumably these are wagons provided by the GWR for the Craigddhu traffic.
(From GWR photographs.)

stopped quickly however great the emergency, so if any animal strayed on to the track, the train was likely to be derailed, and axles, wheels, wagon bodies and slates flung pell-mell aside.

Until 1872, the slate went to Portmadoc Harbour for shipment, but after a yard had been opened at Minffordd for exchange of traffic with the Cambrian Railways, much slate was transhipped to standard gauge wagons and sent off by rail instead of by sea. Then in 1881 the London & North Western Railway, and in 1883 the Great Western, opened branch lines to Blaenau Ffestiniog, giving each a share in the output of the quarries.

Inevitably this affected the future prosperity of the Festiniog Railway.

CHAPTER TWO

MAKING THE MOST OF WELSH NARROW GAUGE IN 1925

In the summer of 1925, my father was told of a small country pub in Wales where the accommodation was comfortable, the food good, and the charges very reasonable: The Goat Hotel at Llanuwchllyn in Merioneth, a mile from the head of Bala Lake in a peaceful country setting. It had the advantage of being easily accessible, for immediately opposite The Goat and separated from it only by the width of a roadway, was Llanuwchllyn station on the Great Western Railway line from Ruabon through Llangollen to Dolgelley (now Dolgellau) where it joined head on the branch of what had been the Cambrian Railways running inland from Barmouth Junction. The railway was to be an important factor in the success of the holiday, as there was a useful service of trains. These were invariably formed of a Dean 0-6-0 locomotive hauling clerestory coaches, some of which were corridors bearing destination boards reading 'Paddington, Birmingham, Shrewsbury, Llangollen, Barmouth & Pwllheli' – pronunciation of the last was beyond us until we reached Wales and were told. I seem to remember one train calling in the early morning, no doubt with mails and newspapers, but otherwise the nights were undisturbed.

There were few other guests: a father with two sons at one time, a Birmingham dentist with his wife and small children at another, but for much of our stay, we had the place to ourselves, and as there was a piano in

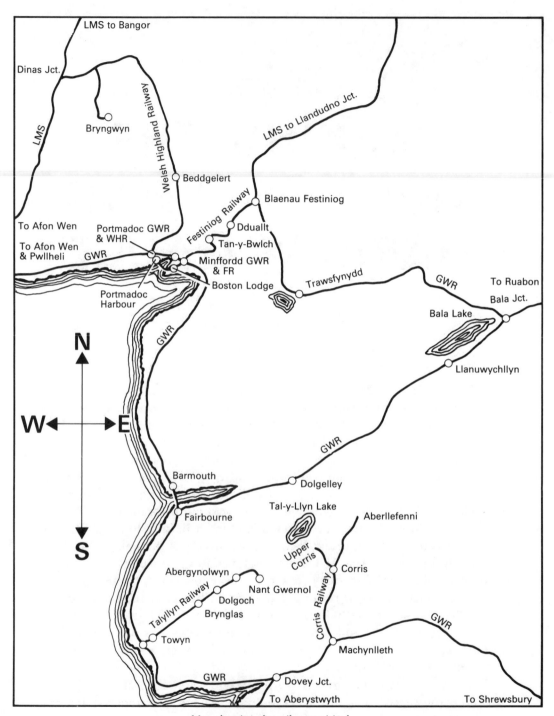

Map showing the railways visited.

the lounge and some old song books, we sometimes made use of those in the evenings.

The food was ample. Every morning of our fortnight's stay there was a dish of fried eggs, bacon, and mushrooms fresh picked from a meadow – and if you wanted a change from all three together, there were half-a-dozen permutations of one or two. The delicious Welsh mutton ('The mountain sheep are sweeter [though] the valley sheep are fatter')⋆ appeared frequently in the evenings with fresh vegetables, a home-made soup and a sweet, and there were always packed lunches available if we wanted to be out for the day. Would that one could find such a place in these days with such excellent simple fare instead of the frozen food so often served tasteless from a microwave.

When Llanuwchllyn had been decided upon, I studied the map closely to see what narrow gauge railways might be within reach. The Festiniog was evidently a certainty, and with luck the journey might be extended to include part of the Welsh Highland; the Talyllyn seemed probable, and on the way from Barmouth Junction to Towyn (now Tywyn) was Fairbourne with a 15in. gauge line from the station through the sand dunes to the Barmouth ferry; but what about the Corris striking north from Machynlleth on the Cambrian route to Aberystwyth? And the Vale of Rheidol from the latter town to Devil's Bridge? What if one were to go east from Llanuwchllyn to Ruabon and south along the GWR Shrewsbury line to Chirk; could out and home and a ride on the Glyn Valley Tramway be fitted into a day?

So maps had to be supplemented with a copy of Bradshaw's fat timetable, which at that date included all these delectable little passenger carrying railways; and information had to be acquired about cheap day tickets and circular tours. The Great Western was generous with both, and one of their tours covered Bala Junction, Blaenau Ffestiniog, the Festiniog Railway to Minffordd, and the GWR thence to Barmouth Junction, Dolgelley and back to Bala Junction, with Llanuwchllyn conveniently on the ring. Another allowed a circular trip from Dolgelley, starting on a GWR charabanc which ran to Tal-y-Llyn Lake, Corris and Machynlleth, with return by rail via Dovey Junction and Barmouth Junction. Bradshaw revealed that the Festiniog journey could be continued over the Welsh Highland as far as Beddgelert; that by quitting the charabanc at Corris and walking up the valley of the Afon Dulas to Aberllefenni, it would be possible to ride from end to end of the Corris Railway's passenger service; that Towyn and the Talyllyn Railway could readily be reached, leaving time to stop off at

⋆ T.L. Peacock: 'The War Song of Dinas Vawr'.

Fairbourne on the way back; and that connecting trains at Ruabon would indeed permit a ride up and down the Glyn Valley Tramway. Only the Vale of Rheidol Railway appeared to be hopelessly out of reach.

Those ventures would account for four days, so there would be plenty of others on which to enjoy the beauty and splendour of the countryside. The roads following the shores of Bala Lake made easy and pleasant walking, as there was little motor traffic at that date. There was the wooded valley of the Afon Lliw, in which an enterprising local engineer had set up a water-wheel that drove a generator and supplied Llanuwchllyn with electric light, then rarely found in rural areas. Our favourite walk was up Cwm Cynllwyd, down which tumbled the Afon Twrch, and where we found a monoglot farmer's wife in neat old fashioned black dress and white apron whom we persuaded by signs to make tea for us. In a kitchen with black leaded range and bright brass and copper, she treated us as her guests, presiding at the table, pouring out the tea, and declining any recompense.

The weather, of course, was very mixed, but though there was plenty of the rain characteristic of the Cambrian Mountains, I have no recollection that it ever confined us indoors for long.

All the narrow gauge railways I have mentioned, with the exception of that at Fairbourne, had been in use in whole or in part for fifty years or more and were still serving the purpose for which they had been built: to carry mineral traffic, predominantly slate, from quarries to an outlet beside sea, river, canal or standard gauge railway. Although they had long since passed the peak of their prosperity owing to road competition and the declining use of Welsh slate, the pride and loyalty of their employees were still strong enough to ensure that whatever defects had developed were not obvious to travellers, so the summer of 1925 was not a bad time to have visited them: a few years later, the picture was a very different one.

Our first excursion was to the Festiniog Railway on 4 August. We had to leave Llanuwchllyn early and change at Bala Junction into the GWR branch train which toiled up through barren mountain lands and over the pass before descending to Trawsfynydd and Blaenau Ffestiniog. We arrived, of course, at the GWR terminus, but it was obviously going to be more interesting to join the narrow gauge train at Duffws, its starting point, where there would be loaded and empty slate wagons filling the sidings at the foot of the two steep cable-operated inclines descending from the quarries. There we found one of the saddle tank locomotives busy with the wagons, the double-boiler Fairlie *Merddin Emrys* (built by the Company at their Boston Lodge Works in 1879) heading the passenger coaches that would form our train, and tank wagons standing in a siding. The station building was a substantial structure of slatestone (what else?) with ashlar

Duffws station as rebuilt in 1869: twin gables of slatestone with ashlar dressings. The double-boiler Fairlie *Merddin Emrys* was at the head of the passenger train, and one of the early 0-4-0 saddle tank locomotives was shunting slate wagons. Tank wagons stood on the right. 4 August 1925.

dressings, rebuilt in 1869 to a pleasing balanced design with twin gables projecting forward from the main block, in front of which a lean-to roof supported on wooden pillars provided shelter for waiting passengers. But the surroundings were grimly industrial, with huge dark grey spoil banks spilling from the back-drop of forbidding mountains.

The weather was doubtful, as it so often is in that mountain region, but I managed to take a good photograph of Duffws station. Passing Glan-y-Pwll Junction, where the branch line serving other quarry inclines trailed in, we ran beside a stream and a row of quarrymen's houses, and over one of the high embankments built with dry-stone near the houses at Tanygrisiau. Beyond, came the spectacular spot where the track rounded a curve on a narrow ledge with a high rock face on the right and a steep drop beyond the supporting wall on the left.

Moelwyn Tunnel, completed at the end of 1842 to replace two temporary inclines, had been designed for nothing larger than the small wagons of the gravity slate trains, long before there was any thought of carrying passengers. The dimensions of coaching stock were therefore very restricted, and clearances so small that doors had to be locked and windows barred. It proved impossible to manoeuvre my bulky reflex camera beneath the bar,

Tan-y-Bwlch on 4 August 1925. *Merddin Emrys* waited on the right hand track as *James Spooner* drew in with a passenger train from Portmadoc.

Tan-y-Bwlch station photographed by F. Frith between 1886 and 1893. The Fairlie *James Spooner* was at the head of the Down train (on the left), and *Merddin Emrys* had the Up train with a tail of empty slate wagons. Beyond the station, the line can be seen, revetted by dry-stone walls, as it climbs the mountain side towards Garnedd Tunnel. *(Photograph: Festiniog Railway.)*

Penrhyndeudraeth, the long level crossing. *Earl of Merioneth* with a train from Porthmadog. The crossing gates were the worse for a collision! 21 July 1987.

Portmadoc Harbour station. *Palmerston*, built in 1864, headed the brake van, two bogie coaches and one of the box-like four-wheelers. *(From a postcard published by the Photochrom Co.)*

but the curves on the mountain side beyond Dduallt were so severe that, riding in the last coach, I was able to take a photograph which showed the locomotive and front of the train.

Then came the great U-shaped loop round Llyn Mair, preserving the descending gradient by keeping close to the 400ft. contour. At Tan-y-Bwlch station, *Merddin Emrys* stopped on the right-hand track, for the Festiniog maintained right-hand running where there was more than one track to run on, and waited to cross an Up train. This was drawn by another Fairlie, *James Spooner*, built by the Avonside Engine Co. in 1872, which announced its approach as it rounded Whistling Curve before drawing into the station. As we descended the lower arm of the U, we could see *James Spooner* well above us at it climbed the other arm on the approach to the short Garnedd Tunnel.

What a contrast between the bleak surroundings of the starting point and the sylvan beauty around Tan-y-Bwlch and Llyn Mair! Thereafter we followed the widening Vale of Ffestiniog, running over the long oblique

Boston Lodge locomotive sheds on 4 August 1925. *Welsh Pony* (1867) was on the right, *Prince* (1863) with steam up outside the corrugated iron extension.

level crossing at Penrhyndeudraeth, stopping at Minffordd where much slate was exchanged with the Cambrian Coast line (by then in the hands of the GWR), passing Boston Lodge Works, and crossing The Cob to Portmadoc Harbour station.

Although J.I.C. Boyd, in his monumental history of the Company, states that in 1923–25 poor maintenance of the locomotives, and the inferior coal then available, sometimes resulted in engine failures and, frequently, in trains running very late, I do not recall any delays in our journey that day. Certainly we were able to do what I had hoped for – travel over the Welsh Highland Railway to and from Beddgelert and still be in time to make the vital connection with the GWR at Minffordd on the homeward leg.

At Portmadoc, there was plenty of time before the Welsh Highland train was due to leave for me to stroll off in search of more photographs. On reaching Boston Lodge, I saw two of the earliest Festiniog locomotives, both built by George England & Co. of London; *Welsh Pony* of 1867 in the two road engine shed built with stone about 1890, and *Prince* of 1863

Train from Portmadoc crossing The Cob on 4 August 1925.

Taliesin, 0-4-4 Fairlie with a single power bogie, built by the Vulcan Foundry in 1896. *(Photograph: Topical Press c. 1923.)*

Festiniog Railway bogie coach with open sides, one of six built by Robert Hudson Ltd., Leeds, in 1923 for £155 each, to a design used by the War Department for light railways on the Western Front during the 1914–18 war. *(Photograph: Topical Press Agency c. 1923.)*

Welsh Pony crossing Portmadoc High Street with a train of Festiniog Railway rolling stock on the way from the Welsh Highland Railway to the Harbour station. In front, ahead of the bogie coaches, were three of the small four-wheeled carriages with very low floors, two with open 'observation' sides and one with glazed windows. 4 August 1925.

standing with steam up outside the corrugated iron extension. As I made my way back, I met one of the double-boiler Fairlies crossing The Cob with an Up train, and even then there was time for me to walk into the town for a view I was very keen to take; that of a train from the Welsh Highland cautiously making its way across Portmadoc High Street on its way to Harbour station.

The Welsh Highland Railway had only been opened two years earlier, on 1 June 1923, followed a week later by the link through Portmadoc, both constructed under Light Railway Orders issued by the Ministry of Transport. But the Welsh Highland incorporated two narrow gauge railways of some age: part of the Croesor Tramway built privately about 1863 as a horse tramway to carry slate from quarries on the west side of the Moelwyn Mountains to the quays of Portmadoc; and the North Wales Narrow Gauge Railway from an exchange station with the London & North Western Railway at Dinas Junction, three miles south of Caernarvon, to Rhyd-ddu (later named South Snowdon), about 3½ miles north of Beddgelert. There was also a branch line from Tryfan Junction to Bryngwyn to serve slate quarries on the flank of Moel Tryfan. The line from Dinas to Rhyd-ddu was the only completed part of a grandiose scheme authorised by Act of 1872 for

Welsh Highland Railway rock cutting north of Nantmor (later Aberglaslyn) station. *(Photograph: Topical Press Agency c. 1923.)*

Unlined rock tunnels in the Pass of Aberglaslyn. *(Photograph: F. Frith, reproduced by the Welsh Highland Railway Society.)*

Beddgelert station. *(Photographed by F. Frith and reproduced by the Welsh Highland Railway Society.)*

the NWNGR to extend from the Croesor line to Beddgelert and thence to Betws-y-Coed, a formidable undertaking through the valleys and over the pass in that mountainous area around Snowdon.

Beyond the Welsh Highland's own station, Portmadoc New, the train crossed the Cambrian Coast line on the level and ran across the meadows bordering the Afon Glaslyn to Croesor Junction, where the line of the old horse tramway could be seen making for the Moelwyn Mountains. Soon the valley narrowed and the spectacular part of the journey began – and spectacular it certainly was through the Pass of Aberglaslyn where the line ran on a shelf hewn from the rock and passed through unlined tunnels, changing sides by a seventy-foot lattice girder span across the foaming waters of the Glaslyn. It was by then very wet, so we made our way to the Royal Goat Hotel in Beddgelert for tea while waiting for a train to take us back. Photography was out of the question, but I was later able to obtain from the Topical Press Agency prints of photographs which had been used to illustrate an article in *The Railway Gazette* in October 1923; scenes showing the line through the Pass only a few months after it had been opened.

I never had the opportunity to travel over the rest of the Welsh Highland Railway, but I doubt whether the run past Quellyn Lake and the foothills of the Snowdon Range could have exceeded in wild beauty that part which I had seen around Aberglaslyn.

The Welsh Highland Railway in the Aberglaslyn Pass threading its way along a shelf hewn in the rock and through a succession of tunnels. The train seen entering a tunnel was drawn by a Festiniog 0-4-0 saddle tank engine, and that leaving a tunnel was headed by a Baldwin 4-6-0 built in 1917 for the War Department and bought by the WHR in 1923. *(From two postcards published by J.E. Powell of Beddgelert.)*

NWNGR 0-6-4 *Moel Tryfan* on train at South Snowdon. *(Photograph: Welsh Highland Railway Society.)*

NWNGR bogie coach built by the Gloucester Wagon Co. in 1877. *(Photograph: Historical Model Railway Society, Gloucester Railway Carriage & Wagon Co. collection.)*

The metamorphosis of the Welsh Highland Railway engine *Russell*! The 2-6-2 tank engine as built by the Hunslet Engine Co. in 1906 for the North Wales Narrow Gauge Railway, which used the Westinghouse brake. *(Photograph: Topical Press Agency c. 1923.)*

Russell's appearance was marred in 1923 when her height was reduced to fit the Festiniog's loading gauge; but even after mutilation her width was too great to pass through the FR tunnels, so she was never able to work through to Blaenau as intended! Vacuum brake had replaced Westinghouse. At Portmadoc 4 August 1925.

Russell as restored to original condition by the Welsh Highland Railway Society, in steam on 18 April 1987, still in works grey but soon to be repainted in maroon livery. *(Photograph: Welsh Highland Railway Society.)*

Snowdon Ranger, Fairlie 0-6-4 side tank engine with a single power bogie, built with her sister *Moel Tryfan* by the Vulcan Foundry for the opening of the North Wales Narrow Gauge Railway in 1877. *(Builder's photograph reproduced by the Welsh Highland Railway Society.)*

CHAPTER THREE

FESTINIOG COLLAPSE AND RECOVERY

The tonnage of slate carried by the Festiniog Railway reached its peak of 139,000 in 1897, and thereafter declined steeply and almost consistently. Increasing use of roof tiles and imported slates reduced the demand for the Welsh product, and with road competition joining that of the LNWR and GWR Blaenau Ffestiniog branch lines, the narrow gauge railway was hard hit. In 1902, earnings were insufficient for a dividend to be paid on the Ordinary Shares, and after 1913 not even on the Preference Shares.

Passenger traffic reached its peak of 208,000 in 1925, but increasing competition by road vehicles, public and private, took its toll thereafter. The decline was arrested in the mid-1930s by a vigorous publicity campaign and the introduction of tourist tickets including the Festiniog and the associated Welsh Highland in circular tours begun and ended on lines of the GWR or LMS. These met with success until the income of the little railways fell so low that maintenance was inadequate, timekeeping suffered, and connection with the standard gauge trains became unreliable.

By June 1939, the tonnage of slate had dropped to a mere 30,000, less than a quarter of what it had been around the turn of the century, while the number of passengers carried was less than a quarter of what it had been in 1925. Soon after the outbreak of war in September, all passenger services, including the quarrymen's trains, were withdrawn, and when, a year after the end of the war, slate trains also ceased to run, it seemed that the end had come. One short section remained in use, however, from the foot of the quarry inclines at Duffws to the exchange sidings with the GWR and LMS, worked by the quarry owners who rented track and wagons from the Festiniog Company.

Sadly, the other narrow gauge Welsh railways I had known were in no better plight. The Glyn Valley Tramway had been abandoned in July 1935. The Welsh Highland and its constituents, which had never realised expectations nor proved commercially viable, ceased to carry passengers in September 1936 and closed altogether at the beginning of June 1937. The Corris ceased passenger carrying at the end of 1930, but it remained open for freight until damaged by floods in August 1948. After that date, the Talyllyn alone remained operative, though limping badly and able to run trains only if it had a locomotive in working order.

Festiniog management, such as it was, had abandoned hope and would gladly have abandoned the railway also, but application to the Ministry of Transport in 1950 for an Abandonment Order brought the unexpected reply that the Ministry had no authority to issue one because the powers granted under the original Act of Parliament could only be annulled by a new Act; this, however, was something the Company was unable to afford! Many felt that a railway of such historic importance, once having had worldwide influence, ought not to be allowed to sink into oblivion without protest: but what could be done?

However, at that very time a praiseworthy effort was being made to save the tottering Talyllyn. A Preservation Society had been formed late in 1950 with the avowed intention of restoring track and rolling stock to a condition able to sustain a regular service, and the outcome, 15,000 passengers during the 1951 season, showed that such a revival was practicable. The beauty of the scenery traversed, the appeal of the narrow gauge as a curiosity, and its access to points no roadway reached, all combined to lure tourists to quit their cars at the terminus in the seaside resort of Towyn (Tywyn) and embark on an intriguing journey.

The Festiniog had much more to offer than the Talyllyn. But revival, and the preliminaries to revival, take time; and meanwhile weeds and trees claimed the unused right-of-way, and rot and rust took possession of many of its structures. The first published suggestion that restoration ought to be undertaken appeared in *The Railway Gazette* of 27 July 1951 in a letter from Heath Humphrys, a seventeen-year-old. Youth, as well as age and experience, was to play a large part in what lay ahead.

Several years passed, however, before Heath Humphrys's letter bore fruit, for although meetings were held in the autumn of 1951 in Bristol and Barnet, it was not until a further gathering, in April 1952 at the London home of the Stephenson Locomotive Society, that a preservation society began to take shape. Among those who became involved were F. Gilbert, a builder, wise and experienced, Allan Garraway, a professional railwayman and engineer, also an accountant, a solicitor, a local government engineer and a banker; some of these had influential friends in engineering and construction companies.

As in the case of the Talyllyn, the old company of proprietors was still in being, but unlike the rescuers of the Talyllyn who had been generously encouraged by the owners, the admirable body of Festiniog supporters found themselves faced by a vestigial management which had no faith in revival. The embryo society was therefore unable to act without acquiring the shares, and although those shares had little value, outright purchase was beyond their means. In June 1954, however, a Holding Company was formed to do this, the bulk of the shares being bought by Alan Pegler with an interest-free loan from his father, and placed in a non-profit making Trust. New management could then be installed in place of the old. But as those who had initiated the movement for preservation had not obtained control of the Company, they found to their chagrin that unless they had expert knowledge or special technical skill, they were limited to providing a pool of volunteer labour instead of taking part in operation as the members of the Talyllyn Preservation Society could do. In December 1954 they

The result of years of neglect: the mass of rhododendrons spread down the sides of the cutting, engulfing the rails where the figure is standing. *(Photograph: J.B. Snell, March 1954).*

therefore formed the entirely separate Festiniog Railway Society whose part was to raise as much money as they could by subscriptions and donations and to hand the amounts over to the Railway Company, in return for which they could appoint a director to represent their interests on the Board.

There were to be found in the Society and in the locality, those whose work would be invaluable. Pre-eminent was Allan Garraway who, in spite of the uncertain future, quit British Railways' employment to become General Manager and Engineer of the Festiniog in June 1955. But there were others, such as Will Jones, formerly the Festiniog's permanent way ganger, who was ready to resume his old tasks, and his wife Bessie, stationmistress at Tan-y-Bwlch in earlier days, who gave a fillip to publicity by reappearing in national costume when the time came to welcome trains at that station once again.

After so many years of neglect, clearing the track of saplings and undergrowth, and making rails and formation fit to bear trains, was a tough undertaking, but it proceeded steadily. Then a far more formidable obstacle unexpectedly appeared, threatening to block for ever complete restoration of the Festiniog line: the British Electricity Authority (later the Central Electricity Generating Board), confident of its power, announced its intention of acquiring by compulsory purchase a part of the Festiniog's right-of-way in order to submerge it in a reservoir. Moreover, compensation for the severance was refused on the ground that the railway had long ceased to operate; which was not strictly accurate because of the short section rented and used by the quarry owners at Blaenau Ffestiniog. Those who wish to follow in detail the legal struggle that ensued between the railway and the electricity authority should read John Winton's book, *Little Wonder*; suffice it to say here that after a battle lasting more than fifteen years, the corporation yielded to its small antagonist's persistence and the railway was awarded compensation for loss of profit, a not inconsiderable sum, because in the meantime trains had run profitably over longer and longer distances as the rails were restored. This sum, augmented in cash and kind by various public bodies and commercial firms, enabled the railway to complete its line, and, in rising above the level of the reservoir, to equip itself with a new Moelwyn Tunnel of greater dimensions to replace the old one drowned in the waters, as well as a feature never before seen in Britain – a spiral loop, completed in 1971.

So the public service, which had begun in July 1955 with no more than the short run across The Cob and had been extended to Tan-y-Bwlch in April 1958 and to Dduallt ten years later, was at last able to reach its goal at Blaenau Ffestiniog, where a new station, shared with British Rail, was brought into use on 23 May 1982, exactly 150 years after the Act of

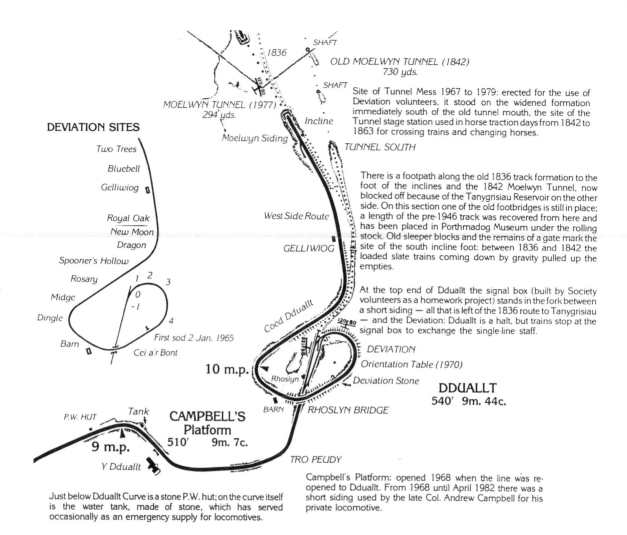

DEVIATION SITES

SHAFT

1836

OLD MOELWYN TUNNEL (1842)
730 yds.

Site of Tunnel Mess 1967 to 1979: erected for the use of Deviation volunteers, it stood on the widened formation immediately south of the old tunnel mouth, the site of the Tunnel stage station used in horse traction days from 1842 to 1863 for crossing trains and changing horses.

SHAFT

MOELWYN TUNNEL (1977)
294 yds.

Incline

TUNNEL SOUTH

Moelwyn Siding

Two Trees

Bluebell

Gelliwiog

Royal Oak

New Moon

Dragon

West Side Route

There is a footpath along the old 1836 track formation to the foot of the inclines and the 1842 Moelwyn Tunnel, now blocked off because of the Tanygrisiau Reservoir on the other side. On this section one of the old footbridges is still in place; a length of the pre-1946 track was recovered from here and has been placed in Porthmadog Museum under the rolling stock. Old sleeper blocks and the remains of a gate mark the site of the south incline foot: between 1836 and 1842 the loaded slate trains coming down by gravity pulled up the empties.

GELLIWIOG

Spooner's Hollow

Rosary

Midge

Dingle

Barn

1 2
0   3
-1
4

First sod 2 Jan. 1965

Cei a'r Bont

Coed Dduallt

At the top end of Dduallt the signal box (built by Society volunteers as a homework project) stands in the fork between a short siding — all that is left of the 1836 route to Tanygrisiau — and the Deviation: Dduallt is a halt, but trains stop at the signal box to exchange the single-line staff.

DEVIATION

Orientation Table (1970)

10 m.p.

Rhoslyn

Deviation Stone

DDUALLT
540' 9m. 44c.

BARN

RHOSLYN BRIDGE

P.W. HUT

Tank

CAMPBELL'S
Platform
510'   9m. 7c.

9 m.p.

Y Dduallt

TRO PEUDY

Campbell's Platform: opened 1968 when the line was re-opened to Dduallt. From 1968 until April 1982 there was a short siding used by the late Col. Andrew Campbell for his private locomotive.

Just below Dduallt Curve is a stone P.W. hut; on the curve itself is the water tank, made of stone, which has served occasionally as an emergency supply for locomotives.

Plan of the spiral at Dduallt leading to the new Moelwyn Tunnel, also showing the abandoned route from Dduallt station to the original tunnel of 1842. *(Reproduced by permission of the Festiniog Railway.)*

incorporation had been passed. The long struggle to re-open the entire route in the teeth of official opposition had, however, given the railway valuable publicity in the national press, which did not fail to report the final success when the new station was reached.

One cannot recapture the thrill of a journey first made over the Festiniog Railway more than sixty years ago, but with the passage of time one's appreciation is certainly sharpened. Of course, no more than any other British railway does the Festiniog now serve its community as it did then, carrying away its produce and supplying its industrial and domestic needs –

machinery, coal, groceries, furnishings, etc. Nevertheless, although depending solely on the tourist trade, the Festiniog is a greal deal more than just another preserved railway. It connects two standard gauge lines of British Rail, the Conwy Valley branch from Llandudno to Blaenau Ffestiniog with the Cambrian Coast Line, both of which offer splendid scenery hidden from the motorist, the first twisting its way through woodland and above a rushing mountain river, the second following a spectacular course between cliffs and the sea. So a journey by the Festiniog can be much more than a trip from end to end and back again as on so many revived lines.

The surveying and engineering of the Festiniog's route is still something to be wondered at. The descent is not now continuous because there is a climb from Tanygrisiau to rise above the reservoir; but it is followed by a fall to the spiral and the station at Dduallt, and the rest of the route is the original one. The most beautiful part is the stretch of three miles between Tan-y-Bwlch and Rhiw Goch, richly afforested with oak, beech, sweet- and horse-chestnuts, as well as ash and silver birch, in addition to the firs. Rhododendrons grow tall, foxgloves flourish, heather gives bright colour to rock faces. There are sinuous curves as the line snakes its way high above the Vale of Ffestiniog with a rock face on one side and, on the other, a steep bank revetted with stone. It runs on top of narrow embankments built of dry-stone – where else was soil so scarce and stone so plentiful that railway embankments were so formed?

Allan Garraway, who had been in it from the first as a volunteer and as General Manager from 1955, had seen the restoration through, aided by a permanent staff that grew from small beginnings to around fifty. But the tremendous task could never have been completed without the work of the volunteers. Some came because hard physical labour, 'pioneering' through the jungle of saplings and undergrowth, provided a welcome change from their normal routine. Others brought specialist knowledge of electricity, welding, carpentry. There were professional men, lawyers, doctors, clergy, army officers, engineers, schoolmasters, and an invaluable body of trained railwaymen, all using their holiday times to help. Many came in groups, organised regionally or by clubs and schools: the very first working party was formed by boys of St Paul's School during their summer holidays in 1954; and there was a succession of younger boys from a North London school brought year after year by Keith Catchpole, who were nicknamed 'Tadpoles' because of their age and their leader's name; carefully briefed before their arrival, their appetite for hard physical toil had nothing of immaturity about it. Perhaps the most remarkable were the 'Deviationists', who built the line between Dduallt and Tanygrisiau with its earthworks and its spiral, and tackled the unglamorous task of clearing spoil from the new

Dduallt, 21 July 1987. *Earl of Merioneth* arriving at the station with the 'Mountain Prince' train from Porthmadog as *Mountaineer*, coming from Blaenau Ffestiniog, descends the spiral and approaches Rhoslyn Bridge.

Tan-y-Bwlch station from the footbridge, 23 July 1987, as *Earl of Merioneth* draws in with the 'Mountain Prince' returning from Blaenau Ffestiniog.

Blaenau Ffestiniog, the new station: BR rails and platform in the foreground, a Festiniog Railway train standing at its own platform on the left. 23 July 1987.

tunnel bored by Cornish miners. A few of these Deviationists were members of the Festiniog Railway Society, but most were not even specially interested in railways: rather, they were keen to meet a challenge or to gain experience of civil engineering. Some were already experienced civil engineers, at least one was an architect, but many were university students or young men and women who had just left school, or members of youth clubs. Some had special skills, others were drawn by the satisfaction of wielding a shovel in work that showed worthwhile results.

Once there was a railway to run, there was work of quite a different kind for some sixty-five volunteers during the summer season, as booking clerks, ticket collectors, buffet car attendants, guards and locomotive firemen. A limited number of the latter subsequently qualified as drivers, amateurs among the full-time professionals, among the latter at one time being the late Bill Hoole, after finishing his career as a top-link East Coast engineman. Two contrasting examples show the spirit pervading Festiniog volunteers today: a retired stockbroker goes each summer to act as signalman; an enterprising local boy, tall for his fourteen years, whose preference is beyond the understanding of his telly-watching contemporaries, likes to help in

Train from Porthmadog leaving Tan-y-Bwlch across a dry-stone embankment on a wintry day early in 1970. At that date the service ran no further than Dduallt. The locomotive was *Blanche*. *(From a card published by the Festiniog Railway reproducing a photograph by Harold Lievesley.)*

Boston Lodge Works after school hours and is a member of the Parks & Gardens section which plants tubs, shrubs and flower beds, achieving outstanding success at Minffordd.

The appearance of the Festiniog today is, of necessity, a mixture of old and new; not least at Porthmadog where new buildings have been added to those of 1878–9 and there are a good refreshment room, a well-stocked shop, a museum and a large car park. The booking office, which holds agencies for British Rail, Sealink, local bus services, cruises by ship and foreign tours by rail, was equipped in 1985 with a fully computerised booking system, the first on a British railway, which enables tickets to be issued far more rapidly than previously. At the end of the day, the computer adds to its own total the cash paid in by guards for tickets issued on trains and that taken at the various sales counters, and displays running totals for the day, week, month and year.

Undoubtedly, the biggest change from the old Festiniog is in the passenger rolling stock. The dimensions of the original Moelwyn Tunnel had severely limited the size of carriages that could be used, so that the

Minffordd station: a pleasant station house, splendid trees, flower beds on the left, plants in tubs on the right. 21 July 1987.

Coaches of the Centenary stock in Tan-y-Bwlch station, 12 May 1986.

four-wheeled 'boxes' of 1863–4 had very low floors and very low roofs. Four still remain, restored so that they can occasionally be pressed into service. The compartment bogie coaches introduced from 1873 onwards had a little more headroom, but there is no doubt that the Centenary stock, built since 1965 to more generous dimensions in anticipation of restoration of services to Blaenau Ffestiniog through the new tunnel, afford the passenger a degree of comfort hitherto unknown on the railway. These include saloon coaches with seats either side of a central aisle; a First Class car with an observation compartment at one end and, at the other, a saloon furnished with armchairs from a Pullman Car; and Buffet Cars. All these new vehicles are capable being interconnected so that a steward can wheel a refreshment trolley from end to end while the train is in motion. All were built by the Company at their Boston Lodge Works.

The locomotive stock is now very varied. To *Prince* of 1863–4 and the Fairlie *Merddin Emrys* of 1879 have been added *Linda* and *Blanche*, both 2-4-0 saddle tank locomotives with tenders, built for the Penrhyn Quarry Railway in 1893 and bought by the Festiniog in 1963; *Mountaineer*, a 2-6-2 tank engine

Observation Car No 10, built at Boston Lodge Works in 1970, seen at Porthmadog on 12 May 1986 at the rear of a train of Centenary coaches.

Pullman Car chairs in coach No 10, the floor covered with a carpet displaying the FR emblem. 23 July 1987.

Blanche, built for the Penrhyn Quarry Railway in 1893 and bought by FR in 1963. Unlike *Linda*, *Blanche* has a tender-cab as protection for the enginemen when running in reverse towards Porthmadog. At Minffordd, 21 July 1987.

Earl of Merioneth, built at Boston Lodge in 1979, with the 'Mountain Prince' at Tan-y-Bwlch, 23 July 1987.

Mountaineer resplendent in fresh paint at Tan-y-Bwlch, 23 July 1987. She was built by the American Locomotive Company for the War Department in 1917, and was given to the FR in 1967.

The armoured Simplex tractor in the yard of Boston Lodge Works, December 1955. Some of the armour had been removed, but enough remained to show the massive construction and suggest the weight. *(Photograph: J.B. Snell.)*

Dduallt Signal Cabin. The electric train staff instruments can be seen on the left. 21 July 1987.

Mountaineer crossing The Cob, 23 July 1987: low tide on the right, reclaimed land on the left.

Blanche drawing into the loop at Tan-y-Bwlch after being held at the Home signal, out of sight round the curve in the cutting. 23 July 1987.

built by the American Locomotive Co. for the War Department in 1917 and given to the Festiniog Railway in 1967; and the new Fairlie *Earl of Merioneth*, completed at Boston Lodge Works in 1979. All the steam engines burn oil instead of coal to reduce the risk of forest fires.

In addition to these, there are eight or nine internal combustion loco-motives. One was built in 1917 by the Motor Rail & Tramcar Co. of Bedford for the War Department as an armoured Simplex tractor with a 40 b.h.p. petrol engine. Bought by the Festiniog in 1923, its supreme performance came during the early stages of line clearance in 1954–5, when its plated body and heavy weight enabled it to be driven at the charge into the undergrowth, uprooting anything in its path. More peacefully, it headed the first passenger train across The Cob in July 1955. A diesel engine has replaced the petrol one, and it has been named *Mary Ann*. The diesels are mostly used on works trains, but three have been fitted with the vacuum brake, and of these, *Upnor Castle*, built in 1954 for the Royal Navy's Chattenden & Upnor Railway near Chatham, is used on the first and last passenger trains of the day from Porthmadog. (Reduced fares are available on the diesel-hauled 'Early Bird').

The Festiniog runs eleven trains a day during the summer peak. There are four passing loops, at Minffordd, Rhiw Goch, Tan-y-Bwlch and Dduallt, each of which is equipped with electric train staff instruments. Ungated level

Tan-y-Bwlch, the approach from Porthmadog, showing the automatically operated point motor in the foreground. The building on the right is the café. 23 July 1987.

crossings have warning lights and sirens actuated by the trains, and a remarkable automatic signalling system, the first of its kind in this country, has recently been installed at Tan-y-Bwlch. There, an approaching train faces a Home colour light signal, where it will be checked if the train it is to pass has already been signalled to enter the loop. As soon as the latter has come to a stand in the station, the signal will clear for the former, and when that also is at a stand, electric motors reverse the points at both exits, and the Starting signals show green. When each train has left, the motors reset the points to their normal position. It is intended to equip Minffordd in the same way in 1988, and the other two loops later if needed.

Once again, the Festiniog points the way!

CHAPTER FOUR

THE TALYLLYN RAILWAY

In 1925, no one could have described the Talyllyn as 'a proper railway'. No doubt it deserves that definition now, after thirty years' work by the Preservation Society. But even in 1925 it had an engaging charm as a period piece, and its route was a beautiful one as it climbed for 6½ miles on a north-easterly course from Towyn (now Tywyn) through wide pastures and along a ledge on the sylvan slopes of the mountains to the south of Cader Idris, threading its way up the narrowing valley of the Afon Fathew to its head. There, a low divide separates the Fathew from the Afon Dysynni flowing from that Tal-y-Llyn Lake from which the railway took its name but never reached. About half a mile beyond the divide the passenger terminus was reached, a quarter of a mile short of, and nearly 150ft. above, the village of Abergynolwyn situated beside the Dysynni. But that was not the end of the line, as the rails ran on along a rock ledge high above the Nant Gwernol ravine and up three inclines rising about 330ft. to reach those slate quarries at Bryn Eglwys which were the reason for building the railway.

When construction began in April 1864, the railway was intended to be a private one for mineral traffic only, to be worked by steam locomotives one of which had already been ordered. A private line of this kind could be built without statutory authority if the land it traversed belonged to the promoters or to landowners who had granted way-leave. The promoters soon decided, however, to make it a public railway carrying passengers, and for this Parliamentary approval was necessary, so a Bill was introduced and the Talyllyn Railway incorporated by an Act of July 1865.

The first locomotive had been delivered in the autumn of 1864, and about the time the Act was passed, the rails had been laid to Abergynolwyn, so it seems possible that structures such as bridges over the line had been designed when the only vehicles expected to pass through them were the engine and narrow wagons. When Captain H.W. Tyler (later Sir Henry Tyler), who had inspected and encouraged the Festiniog Railway, came in September 1866 to examine the line before passenger trains could be allowed to run, he commented on the limited clearance between the sides of the carriages and the bridge abutments, and added that the management had therefore decided to slew the rails to one side under each arch, and permanently fasten the doors and bar the windows on that side of the carriages, conditions which still apply today. He recommended improvements to the permanent way, fencing and hedging, and remarked on the unsteady riding of the engine, but when he reported early in November after making a second inspection (riding on the engine 'at a speed of 20 miles an hour'!), he expressed the opinion 'that this little line may be opened without danger to the public using it'.* So passenger trains began to run in December 1866.

Quarrying at Bryn Eglwys had begun about 1847, yielding slate of excellent quality, but as it had to be won from underground workings and carried by pack-horses to Aberdovey, a port just over three miles south-east of Towyn, heavy expense was incurred before it could be shipped to its destination. Unfortunately, when quarrying was extended after the railway was built, there proved to be less of the good slate than had been expected, and only one new site that yielded really good material, but as that split into slates so thick and heavy that they could be carried only by the strong timbers of large buildings, the market for them was very limited. By 1911 working had proved uneconomic, and the quarries were therefore closed.

Almost immediately, however, they were leased by Henry Hayden Jones, MP for Merioneth 1911–1945, who re-opened them in order to provide local employment, subsidising the losses from his own pocket. In 1925 there was work for 160 men, but the workings became dangerous as well as unprofitable, and in 1948 production finally ceased. Nevertheless, Sir Hayden kept the railway running for the sake of the little community at Abergynolwyn and the visitors to the growing seaside town of Towyn, as well as the tourists who had been coming in increasing numbers since the last years of the nineteenth century, drawn by the beauty of the area, notably the Dolgoch Falls and Tal-y-Llyn Lake, with the stout hearted walking the three miles from the terminus to the lake, the less energetic riding in a horsedrawn brake or, later, motor charabanc.

Meantime, as Sir Hayden had little money to spare for maintenance, deterioration of the railway steadily increased and services sometimes had to be suspended for days on end because no locomotive was in working order. When he died in 1950, closure appeared inevitable until Tom Rolt gathered

* Rolt, L.T.C., *Railway Adventure*, p. 13, quoting from the Report.

round him a group of like-minded enthusiasts who determined to keep the railway running, and succeeded in winning the support of Sir Hayden's executors.

The railway they saved has three valid claims to fame. In the first place, when it was opened towards the end of 1866 it was the first narrow gauge railway in Britain – and that almost certainly means in the world – to have been *designed* for operation by steam locomotives, as the earlier narrow gauge lines in Wales had all begun as horse-worked mineral tramways. As it was only two years since the Festiniog had adopted steam traction and passenger carrying, this was a bold move.

Secondly, the two four-coupled locomotives and five four-wheeled coaching vehicles acquired in 1864–7 were the only stock in use, apart from wagons, not only in 1925, but also when the Preservation Society was formed in 1951, so that the Talyllyn was a unique example of a railway of the

Towyn Pendre station, 10 August 1925. The shed was of the same pattern as that at Abergynolwyn, but in rather better condition!

mid-1860s, surviving intact and unaltered for more than eighty years, even in its primitive and wayward operating methods. Its third claim is, of course, that it was the first of many railways of various gauges to be rescued or 'preserved' by an association of interested amateurs.

However, it is impossible to 'preserve' a railway in the sense that a Government department preserves a ruined castle or monastery, by arresting further decay, because a railway has to renew working parts and structures in order to remain operational. Hence the Talyllyn has improved its track and, like the Festiniog and the Welshpool & Llanfair, acquired additional locomotives and coaches from a variety of sources, so that it now bears little resemblance to the railway I visited on 10 August 1925.

The day my father and I travelled via Dolgelley and Barmouth Junction to Towyn and thence up the Talyllyn was wet, with a difficult light for photography. There were then three regular trains a day in summer, one leaving Towyn Wharf, where traffic was exchanged with the GWR, in the morning, another in the afternoon, and a third in the early evening. There was also an early morning service on Mondays for quarrymen only; and another on Saturday evenings, no doubt taking village shoppers home and carrying country walkers back. The winter service was two trains each way daily. We caught the afternoon train from Towyn Pendre station, Wharf not then being officially a passenger station. I noted that the line ran between thick and high hedges through gently rising country to Rhyd-yr-onen, steepening thereafter as it made its way up the side of the valley of the Afon Fathew and through woods to Dolgoch, beyond which trees were scarce as the line approached the valley head and struck across to the Dysynni. It was not a comfortable ride: 'The track is rather lightly laid,' I wrote, 'and in many places the rails have sunk, producing a marked effect on the train.' As some of the rail joints were supported in a chair but not fishplated, the carriages pitched on passing over them! Moreover, 'heavy super-elevation on the curves, exaggerated by the narrowness of the gauge and the overhang of the carriages, gave the traveller an unpleasant tendency to slip sideways on the wooden seats' – that was in the Third Class; First Class seats had a blue covering of some kind which kept superior passengers in place.

The locomotive was the well known No 1, *Talyllyn*, built by Fletcher Jennings & Co. at Whitehaven in 1864 as an 0-4-0 saddle tank, but because of her tendency to pitch and yaw, damaging the track, she was very soon returned to the builders to be fitted with a pair of trailing wheels. No 2, *Dolgoch*, also an 0-4-0 but with a tank at the back of the footplate, was built by the same firm the following year. Each engine had cylinders 8in. diameter with a stroke of 16in., driving wheels 2ft. 3in. diameter, and a boiler working at a pressure of 100 lb. per sq. in.; *Talyllyn*'s heating surface was

No 1 *Talyllyn* at Towyn Pendre, 10 August 1925. She was built by Fletcher Jennings & Co., Whitehaven, in 1864 as an 0-4-0 saddle tank, but soon acquired a pair of trailing wheels to steady her movement. At the side of the cab can be seen the scratch-built wooden door used in inclement weather.

No 2 *Dolgoch*, built by Fletcher Jennings & Co. in 1865, at Abergynolwyn, 23 July 1987.

156 sq. ft., *Dolgoch*'s 128. The footplate of both locomotives had a back sheet but no cab when built, a considerable disadvantage that was soon remedied. On the occasion of my visit, *Dolgoch* was under repair in the workshop at Towyn Pendre. This, which is shown in the photograph on page 86, has been described by one who knew it well as 'reasonably well-equipped for maintenance work', with a small furnace for brass founding, a primitive home-made lathe, a drill and a circular saw, which were driven by a small engine drawing steam from the boiler of whichever locomotive was available. ★

Four of the five coaching vehicles formed our train; two Third Class, one First and Third composite, and a van. Together with the fifth, a First Class coach standing at Towyn Pendre, all had 'recently been smartly painted crimson with yellow lining and lettering'. The leading one had straight sides and had been built by the Lancaster Wagon Co. in 1867. The two others, and also the First Class carriage standing idle, had been delivered earlier by Brown Marshalls & Co. of Birmingham, and were better looking with shapely sides – 'more modern looking' was a contemporary comment! The van, which for a few years at the beginning of the twentieth century carried His Majesty's Mails, was also from Brown Marshalls and originally had a veranda at one end for the guard to operate the handbrake. This was enclosed about 1900, provided with duckets (projecting lookouts) for the guard, and acquired an unusual distinction as a travelling ticket office, the guard having to issue tickets at the intermediate stations, none of which had booking offices. So a pigeon-hole window was cut in the ducket, but on the north side only, the side on which all platforms were situated. Unusually for a narrow gauge railway (the Talyllyn's gauge is 2ft. 3in.), the vehicles were provided with side buffers and hook-and-link couplings, but there was no continuous brake, or lighting, or heating – one pities the quarrymen riding the 6 a.m. train in the depth of winter. There was no signalling, the single track being worked on the principle of one-engine-in-steam, but surprisingly there was no telegraph, let alone a telephone circuit. So once a train had ambled off from Towyn at its permitted maximum speed of 10 to 15 mph, there was no news of it until its return, or the arrival of a messenger on foot to report where and why it had been stranded.

In most of this, however, the Talyllyn was little different from the main line railways of the mid-1860s, on which most coaches were four-wheeled with Third Class seats of bare wood, unheated except by foot-warmers, and without continuous brakes, which were not then available. As for contemporary signalling, although the electric telegraph had been in railway use for

★ *Talyllyn Century*, Chapter Four, by J.H.L. Bate.

The First Class coach built by Brown Marshalls & Co. of Birmingham. At Pendre, 10 August 1925.

Collecting tickets at Dolgoch station, 10 August 1925. The pigeon-hole window in the ducket of the guard's van, from which tickets were issued, is visible on the right.

more than twenty years, another twenty were to elapse before the block telegraph system superseded the time interval method for regulating the passage of trains. The principle of one-engine-in-steam, however, long remained a widely accepted method, sometimes still used, of operating single track branch lines. The Talyllyn had therefore been 'a proper railway' in 1866, which indeed was only to be expected as it had been surveyed and built by one of the Spooner family, James Swinton Spooner, son of James Spooner and brother of Charles Easton Spooner, the two who built the Festiniog. The remarkable feature of the Talyllyn was that it remained unchanged, and this was because the declining slate traffic and diminished earnings meant that there was neither need nor means to modernise; the locals, and the tourists, could put up with its archaic equipment for the forty-five minutes the journey took. The wonder was that it remained serviceable for so long, and that was largely due to Edward Thomas who had joined the staff in 1897 and from 1911 to 1950 managed the railway for Sir Hayden Jones.

Filling *Talyllyn*'s saddle tank with water diverted from a stream which flowed down the mountainside and under the mineral line in the Nant Gwernol ravine. 10 August 1925.

After the morning and afternoon trains had reached Abergynolwyn, the coaches stood for an hour or more before the return journey, while the locomotive took empty wagons to the foot of the quarry incline, shunted the sidings, and returned with laden wagons. As the driver of No 1 realised my keen interest, he invited me to ride on the footplate with him.

Understandably, the track was rougher and the curves sharper as the line wound its way picturesquely through the woods and along the narrow shelf cut in the valley flank, high above Nant Gwernol. The engine presently stopped in order to refill the saddle tank by an extraordinarily primitive method, quite unlike that so often photographed in recent years at Dolgoch, where a tank stands on a well-built slatestone base. Here, however, water from one of the streams falling down the mountainside and flowing under the track had been diverted into a wooden trough supported by a roughly built pillar, and fitted with a pipe discharging the water vertically to run away beneath slate slabs under the rails. When the engine drew up, a loose piece of trough kept at the lineside was laid across from a ledge on the pillar to the saddle tank, which was gradually filled while much water cascaded to

Abergynolwyn village: clearly visible is the incline descending from the shed which covered the winding drum. *(From a card in the Talyllyn Railway Historical Series.)*

the ground; a simple and effective way as long as the supply was unlimited! It must have been a good deal more difficult to fill *Dolgoch*'s tank through the pipe projecting from the rear of the cab.

Further on was the winding drum at the head of the steep incline by which supplies reached the village of Abergynolwyn far below, where they were delivered almost to the doors of the houses from wagons running on sidings laid along the streets, surely a unique feature of the Talyllyn Railway, and a boon to the inhabitants of such a remote spot.

Here, the track swung from north-east to south-east up Nant Gwernol to the fan of sidings on a widened shelf at the foot of the first of the quarry inclines. A mountain stream passing beneath had cut a deep and narrow gorge into which it plunged with a ceaseless roar, fitting music to mark the tomb of runaway wagons which, more than once, had leapt from the incline foot.

Very wisely, the Preservation Society decided from the first that the mineral extension from Abergynolwyn must sometime be re-opened so that tourists would be able to enjoy the most spectacular part of the entire line, but it was October 1970 before it became financially possible to begin making it suitable for passenger trains. Much had to be done: the narrow shelf bordered by the steep drop to the Nant Gwernol had to be widened in places; two knuckles of rock round which the track turned sharply had to be blasted to ease the curve; and a station, to be named Nant Gwernol, had to be built once the site of the sidings had been cleared and the retaining wall supporting its outer edge repaired and strengthened. So it was May 1976 before the extension could be brought into use.

Rehabilitation of the Talyllyn showed what could be done to save a railway of historic interest. Quite independently, Heath Humphrys had proposed a Festiniog Railway Preservation Scheme in 1950, but he was then only sixteen years old, and although the seed he planted was tended by other hands and later bore abundant fruit, a personality of greater stature was needed to establish the preservation movement on secure foundations. That was done by Tom Rolt, already widely known as the author of books about canals and as an advocate of waterway restoration. Moreover, being a trained engineer, he was qualified to form a realistic appreciation of what railway rehabilitation involved. Without his leadership, the Talyllyn would never have been saved, and it may be that railway preservation, which has given such pleasure to so many, would have been stillborn.

Of course, the Talyllyn Railway of today is not the Talyllyn of 1866 or 1925 or even 1951. There are purists who deplore this, even some who disapproved of the extension of passenger services to Nant Gwernol. That is an absurd attitude: the old H.M. Office of Works, later the Ministry of the

Nant Gwernol: the sidings at the foot of the first incline leading to the slate quarries. 10 August 1925.

Nant Gwernol station on 22 July 1987, from the foot of the former incline. The difference in the curvature shows that a lot of rock had to be removed to the left of where No 1 was standing in 1925.

Environment, whose preservation of ruined buildings was rightly conservative, would replace fallen stonework that was in good condition when its original position was known; and cathedral chapters employ masons to carve new pinnacles to stand in place of old ones fallen or decayed.

When the Preservation Society took charge in 1951, *Talyllyn* had been out of service for six years, and the condition of *Dolgoch* was such that no one could foretell how much longer she would be able to work before having to be withdrawn for heavy repairs. Not many miles away, two locomotives of the Corris Railway had stood shrouded by tarpaulins since closure of that line in 1948; the elder of the two, built in 1878, was in working order, but the younger, of 1921, had been worked hard and taken out of traffic in 1947 because of the state of her boiler.* It proved possible to buy the two cheaply from British Railways, and it was hoped that the elder would provide relief for *Dolgoch*, whose failure would otherwise have caused a prolonged stoppage which might well have been fatal to the Preservation Society's hopes. The veteran became Talyllyn No 3 and acquired the name *Sir Hayden*, the other becoming No 4 *Edward Thomas*. *Sir Hayden*, however, had narrow wheel treads which led to repeated derailments on the poor track, and had therefore to be withdrawn until the line could be improved, so *Dolgoch* still had to soldier on alone.

Fortunately, news of the rescue of the Talyllyn had aroused interest far and wide. Volunteers had come forward prepared to be trained and do any work during their holidays, and industrial firms offered their services free, the Hunslet Engine Co. of Leeds undertaking overhaul of *Edward Thomas* which had been built by a firm they had absorbed. She was returned to service in June 1952; in 1958 she attracted interest – and unfavourable comment – through being fitted with a Giesl Ejector and an extremely ugly chimney like a funnel with flattened sides, but as the vaunted promises of improved efficiency and economy were not fulfilled, the original chimney was subsequently replaced. The engineering firm Abelson & Co. presented a 2ft. gauge well tank locomotive built by Andrew Barclay & Co. at Kilmarnock in 1918 for the Air Service Construction Corps: an 0-4-0 with 1ft. 10in. driving wheels, cylinders $6\frac{3}{4} \times 10\frac{2}{3}$in., heating surface 115 sq. ft., and working pressure 160 lb. per sq. in. Numbered 6 and named *Douglas* at the donors' request, she arrived at Tywyn in July 1954 after being regauged.

It was then safe to send Nos 1 and 2 for repair as means permitted. *Dolgoch* went first, to Hunt Brothers of Oldbury, in 1954, but it was 1963 before she returned. *Talyllyn* followed in 1957, but was far from satisfactory when she came back (from a different firm) in 1958 and so had to be rebuilt again, this

* The Corris locomotives are described in Chapter Five, page 101.

Douglas at Tywyn Wharf, 22 July 1987. She was built by Andrew Barclay & Co. in 1918 and rebuilt by Hunt Brothers Ltd. in 1954.

time by the railway's own engineering staff at Pendre in 1972. Both retain their original appearance but very little of their original material! A sixth steam locomotive, basically an Andrew Barclay built for the Irish Turf Board in 1949, is under construction at Pendre, but as the existing stud is able to handle the traffic at present offering, there is no urgency to complete it.

Diesels, so quickly available for work and consuming no fuel when standing idle, have been in use for some time as shunters at Tywyn and for drawing engineers' and permanent way maintenance trains. No 5 on the locomotive list, a Ruston & Hornsby of 1940 with a 53 b.h.p. engine and three-speed gearbox, was acquired in 1957 from a Nuneaton quarry company, regauged and named *Midlander*; she has since been rebuilt with a more modern engine, and other parts from a sister locomotive. No 9 is an interesting machine built by Hunslet in 1950 for the National Coal Board for work underground, and therefore is of very limited height; two of these locomotives were obtained in 1970, the second to provide spare parts; with a 75 b.h.p. engine, two-speed mechanical drive through a jackshaft, and a top speed of 8¾ mph, *Alf* is very useful for hauling heavy works trains. No 8, *Merseysider*, is a synthesis of two Ruston & Hornsby 50|b.h.p. locomotives

The three diesels at Pendre, 22 July 1987: *Alf*, the ex-NCB mines locomotive built in 1950 by the Hunslet Engine Co. with a 75 b.h.p. engine and mechanical drive through a jackshaft; *Merseysider*, built by Ruston & Hornsby in 1964, 50 b.h.p. with Dowty Hydrostatic drive; the third, almost hidden, is *Midlander*.

Toby, the Permanent Way Department motor trolley built in 1954, and originally fitted with an Austin Seven engine. At Pendre, 22 July 1987.

built in 1964 for a steel works which closed in 1967. Acquired by the Talyllyn Railway two years later, No 8 was regauged from 3ft. to 2ft. 3in., revivified by transplants from her sister and fitted with an improved cab and exhaust chimney. Dowty Hydrostatic drive enables her to reach 13 mph and so haul passenger trains in times of need, and also to run continuously at a low speed, towing grass-cutting or hedge-trimming machines – very valuable qualities.

It was not only the locomotive stock that had to be augmented by the Preservation Society. At first, there were only the four aged four-wheelers to carry the tourists, and of these, that built by the Lancaster Wagon Co. was behaving so oddly that it had been nicknamed 'Limping Lulu'! Two primitive four-wheeled quarrymen's carriages from the Penrhyn Quarry Railway were presented towards the end of 1952, but these had neither doors nor roofs; one was fitted with a roof, but neither lasted long. Another four four-wheelers, roofed but with open sides, were built at Pendre in 1955–66, some using parts from other Penrhyn vehicles; and two bodies from the Glyn Valley Tramway were rescued and carefully restored in some style as First Class carriages, complete with fully upholstered seats, carpets and luggage racks. But anyone who has travelled in four-wheelers knows that their riding is not particularly smooth!

The Festiniog had shown the better way, with bogie coaches in 1871, and so had the Corris Railway in 1888–98. The body of one of the latter was indeed retrieved for use on the Talyllyn, but 'restoration' turned into rebuilding as a replica, an expensive and time-consuming task. However, a decision to build new Talyllyn coaches on bogie underframes was made in 1959, and between 1965 and 1981 nine entered traffic, the first built by volunteers in the Midlands on an underframe made at Pendre, but to speed up the work, the bodies of seven were constructed by R. Tisdale & Co. of Kenilworth and mounted on underframes also built commercially but fitted with Pendre bogies. The last to be finished was a complete rebuilding at Tywyn of a vehicle bought in 1957 for £25. Some coaches have three or four compartments and space for a guard, though most have six compartments, each capable of seating eight passengers.

For the slate traffic, the old Talyllyn Railway had a hundred wagons of the usual type with slatted sides, and a special van to carry the gunpowder used in the quarries. But there were also open wagons, vans and iron coal wagons to supply the local inhabitants, chiefly the villagers of Abergynolwyn, and, as their supplies had to be lowered down the incline, there were some special iron wagons with one end much higher than the other to prevent loss of coal while descending (two such wagons can be seen in the photograph I took at Nant Gwernol in 1925). As scarcely more than sixteen original wagons remained in 1951, the eleven surviving Corris vehicles were bought, BR parting with them for as little as 10s. each, perhaps thankful to get even that! Others were acquired from various sources, including the Festiniog Railway; some had to be regauged and many rebuilt. There are now forty-six for use in construction, maintenance, and to carry locomotive coal from Tywyn Wharf to the depot at Pendre: sixteen side tipping skips, five hopper wagons, eleven open ones with end-doors, eleven flat wagons, and three with bolsters to carry rails, etc.

Obviously, a railway now entirely dependent on a growing tourist trade could not be operated as the old Talyllyn had been: one engine in steam, points worked by weighted levers set by hand, no signalling, not even a telephone. It was essential that points on the running line should be controlled from a lever frame and secured by facing point locks. There had to be passing loops, and effective single line working between them. A Signals & Telegraph Department began installing telephone equipment in the 1950s, and there is now a fully automatic system enabling train movements to be reported to a controller. The original 40 lb. per yard rails still in position in 1951 were replaced by secondhand rails and sleepers in better condition; these in turn have been succeeded by new rails, mostly 45 and 50 lb., laid on Jarrah hardwood sleepers well-ballasted.

The first passing loop had been provided at Brynglas by 1953, followed by another between there and Abergynolwyn, at Quarry Siding where there is a signal cabin but no station. Colonel McMullen, inspecting the line before giving the Preservation Society authority to run passenger trains, recommended that a single line train staff should be carried by the driver. Soon there were two wooden staffs, one for use between Pendre and Abergynolwyn, the other for the short section between Pendre and Wharf to enable movement of locomotives and rolling stock to and from the depot while a train was proceeding to the upper terminus. With the opening of the Brynglas loop, three were necessary and metal replaced wood, each staff having detachable ends so that the 'staff and ticket' system could be introduced, allowing one train to follow another through the section, the first carrying the end (or 'ticket') applying to the direction of travel, the second taking the staff itself. With the growth of traffic, greater flexibility was needed, and electric train staff instruments were installed, first at Wharf and Pendre and later at Brynglas, Quarry and Abergynolwyn as well.

The Abergynolwyn–Nant Gwernol section is normally occupied by only one train at a time, so the 'staff and ticket' method applies; there is a run-round loop and siding at the end. Abergynolwyn, previously the terminus, had to be considerably developed, with a greatly lengthened platform, 620ft. long, to accommodate two trains simultaneously: that

Abergynolwyn 22 July 1987. The gabled roof of the station building just shows above the platform canopy, on the near side of which, in the open, are tables and benches. Bogie coach No 9, built in 1967, is at the rear end of the train bound for Tywyn standing alongside the western extension of the platform. The signal cabin shows beyond the canopy.

proceeding to Tywyn drawing up alongside the new western end, that for Nant Gwernol passing it in the loop (which extends to the middle of the platform) and stopping at the site of the original station beyond. Because the station is on a curve, obscuring the view of one end from the other, colour light signals have been installed and a signal cabin erected with a 14-lever frame to control all points and signals. The ramshackle wooden shelter had been replaced in 1940, but in 1969 a far better building of slatestone was provided, with a platform canopy, a booking office and a refreshment room. There are also seats and tables in the open at which sandwiches can be enjoyed in fine weather.

Under the direction of the Chief Engineer, J.H.L. Bate, the depot at Pendre has been greatly enlarged. The original slatestone building, which included workshop, engine shed and driver's cottage, is still there, but the cottage now forms part of the shed to house the increased number of locomotives; a forward extension from the workshop is a carriage shed. The

The Workshop in 1987. The old furnace and its chimney-breast can be seen at the back. Repair of the child's pushchair shows that outside work is undertaken!

shop has been re-equipped so that engines and rolling stock can be built and repaired, and even some outside work undertaken, an asset to the town as well as to railway revenue. There are also other carriage sheds and a paint shop, but built of less attractive material than the native slatestone!

Locomotives and rolling stock are smartly maintained: locomotives shine in bronze-green livery with yellow lining and black borders, bright red buffer beams and motion; coaches are clean and conspicuous with cherry-red panels between framing of mid-brown, black underframes and bogies, and yellow axleboxes to denote roller bearings.

All in all, the Talyllyn of today appears in good heart, and if less picturesque than it once was, certainly safer, more comfortable and more lively. One curious anomaly of 1866 survives, however: the trains still have no automatic continuous brake. This has been accepted hitherto because of the low speeds and efficient locomotive braking, but in 1986 there came the opportunity to acquire from an Australian railway Westinghouse air brake equipment for the cost of packing and shipment. It is now at Pendre and before long will be fitted.

What will the purists say when this last peculiarity of the old Talyllyn disappears?

The workshop at Towyn Pendre, 10 August 1925. The photograph shows the furnace, an assortment of parts lying haphazardly on the bench, an array of tools in two wall-racks, and the fitter himself just visible on the extreme left. *Dolgoch* was under repair.

At Abergynolwyn station, 10 August 1925. The leading coach behind *Talyllyn* was that built by the Lancaster Wagon Co., followed by two of the Brown Marshalls & Co. 'more modern looking' coaches and the van, with the guard's ducket showing clearly.

CHAPTER FIVE

THE
CORRIS RAILWAY

Of all the narrow gauge passenger-carrying railways I have known, the Festiniog stood head and shoulders above the others on the grounds of the excellence of its engineering, the solidity of its formation and track, its powerful locomotives of distinctive design, and its bogie coaches. The Vale of Rheidol, which I did not visit until 1946, ran it close, and so also did the Lynton & Barnstaple. The Talyllyn was quaint, and so too, though in a different way, was the short-lived Sand Hutton Light Railway in Yorkshire; another period piece perhaps, but of the 1920s rather than the 1860s. The Glyn Valley was a true tramway, an intriguing example of a roadside railway more common on the Continent than in Britain. The Fairbourne was a useful miniature, and the Ravenglass & Eskdale of the mid-1920s an impressively purposeful one.

The Corris had no special features except for remarkable enterprise in running connecting road services and the provision of a station covered by an overall roof, the like of which was, I believe, to be seen on no other narrow gauge railway in Britain (I remember seeing one equally imposing in Brittany). Yet the Corris had an intimacy and an indefinable charm felt, according to J.I.C. Boyd,* by many besides myself. Although I made but one journey on it and that in one direction only, the Corris caught my fancy, and after all these years it remains one I remember with great affection: a line running in its upper reaches between stone walls amid bare hillsides and, lower down, curving wildly amid surroundings of great beauty between a sylvan river bank and a road through a narrow valley with thickly timbered flanks.

---

* Boyd, J.I.C., *Narrow Gauge Rails in Mid-Wales*, Oakwood Press, 1952, p. 2.

Corris station and carriage shed, 7 August 1925. The brake van and wagons on the right were standing on the avoiding line, which ran round the back of the sheds and rejoined the track to Aberllefenni beyond.

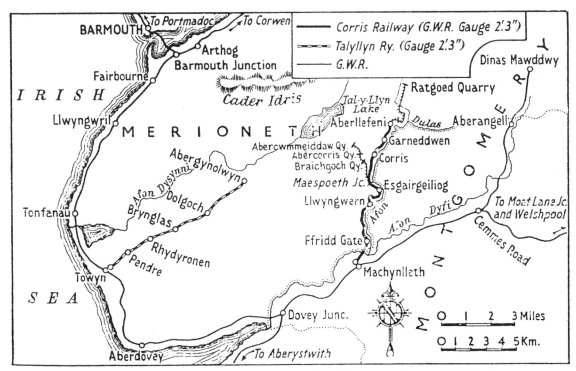

Sketch map of the Corris Railway and neighbouring lines (*The Railway Magazine Vol. 87, 1941, p. 269*).

It appears to have received less attention in print than the others I have mentioned. After my visit on 7 August 1925 I wrote an article which was published in *The Locomotive, Railway Carriage & Wagon Review*. Articles by others appeared in various issues of *The Railway Magazine*; Boyd gave it a chapter in *Narrow Gauge Rails in Mid-Wales (1952)*; and George Behrend has a brief description of its last days in *Gone With Regret*. But the only monograph is that by Lewis Cousins (1949, reprinted 1972), and it is evident that he did not have access to the small but valuable collection of original material preserved by the Great Western Railway and now lodged in the Public Record Office at Kew.

Like many of the other Welsh narrow gauge railways, the Corris began as a horse tramway between quarries and a point of shipment. It was authorised by an Act of 12 July 1858 to extend from slate quarries around Corris and Aberllefenni down the valley of the Afon Dulas to the town of Machynlleth (near which the Dulas flows into the Afon Dyfi or Dovey), and some 2½ miles beyond there to quays on the left bank of the Dovey at Derwenlas.

It was opened on 30 April 1859 as the Corris, Machynlleth & River Dovey Tramroad, gauge 2ft. 3in., but after the Aberystwyth & Welsh Coast Railway (soon to be a constituent of the Cambrian Railways) reached Machynlleth at the beginning of July 1863, slate could be transhipped from narrow to standard gauge at that station, whereafter shipment from the River Dovey Quays became so rare that a year later authority was obtained to abandon the line beyond Machynlleth. At the same time, the cumbersome name was changed to the simple title Corris Railway Company. As finally established, it was eleven miles long, following the shape of a wriggling letter Y, the base at Machynlleth and the fork at Maespoeth Junction, about three-quarters of a mile below Corris station, whence the main line continued north-eastwards by the Dulas to Aberllefenni and beyond, and the branch began to climb the valley side before turning off north-westwards to follow the Afon Deri to a terminus at Upper Corris, about a mile and a half south-east of Tal-y-Llyn Lake.

Although the Act of 1864 authorised the use of steam locomotives, there was no haste to introduce them, and for another nineteen years trains of laden slate wagons continued to run down by gravity, the empties being hauled back by horses – passengers were carried unofficially. In 1878, however, the Company's prospects were transformed by an unexpected development.

In the second half of the nineteenth century, street tramways were laid down in many towns and cities in Britain and other parts of the world, the cars drawn by horses or steam tram engines heavily disguised to avoid scaring the ubiquitous animals frequenting the roadways in herds or between shafts. Over the years, many of these tramways were promoted or acquired by holding companies whose interests included generation of electricity for light and power, and which were therefore eager to spread the use of electric traction. By far the largest of these was the British Electric Traction Company formed in 1895, but another large concern was the Imperial Tramways Company incorporated in 1878 with its headquarters in Bristol; and under the direction of J. Clifton Robinson, three of that company's systems (in Bristol, Middlesbrough and West London) were among the earliest street tramways to be electrified.★ Surprisingly, Imperial Tramways bought the Corris Railway in November 1878, and Clifton Robinson later became its Managing Director and Chairman. Imperial Tramways was not alone in acquiring minor railways; the BET group subsequently included the Swansea & Mumbles (the ancient Oystermouth Railway of 1804) and the Bideford Westward Ho! & Appledore Railway of 1901; among the associations of another group was the North Wales Power & Electric Traction Company with an interest in the projected Portmadoc Beddgelert & South Snowdon Railway. Electrification of the Corris was mentioned, probably not for the first time, in correspondence with Sir Clifton Robinson in 1908; the Portmadoc Beddgelert & South Snowdon Act of 1904 intended the use of electricity; and the Swansea & Mumbles, which had displaced horses by steam in 1893, was electrified in 1929.

It was probably the dynamic direction of the Imperial Tramways Company that impelled the Corris management to make use of their existing authority to introduce locomotives, and to evolve from a mineral tramway into a public railway serving the community. Before engines could be used, however, the light cast iron rails had to be replaced by heavier flat-bottomed steel rails, and before passengers could be carried officially Parliamentary authority had to be obtained. But such a development was not to the liking of the quarry owners, who feared that passenger trains would impede the flow of their mineral traffic. No doubt they failed to realise that the use of locomotives would increase the capacity of the railway. On the other hand, the railway company certainly underestimated the strength and influence of the opposition, for they took delivery of engines and carriages in November 1878 before applying to Parliament, and when they introduced a Bill the following year, it was rejected.

Three outside cylinder 0-4-0 saddle tank locomotives were supplied by the Hughes Engine Co. of Loughborough, later known as the Falcon Engine &

★ The Portrush & Giant's Causeway Tramway of 1883 was the first in the British Isles to operate electric tramcars; current was drawn from overhead wires.

Car Works and later still as the Brush Electrical Co. The same firm built ten small four-wheeled passenger vehicles, which were in fact typical single deck tramcars with longitudinal seats and end doors opening to balconies at each end, where, as on a horsedrawn street car, a driver would stand beside a revolving brake handle. Six of the cars had plain wooden seats for Third Class passengers, and four were upholstered for First Class. ★

Soon after these had been delivered, they were set to use drawn by horses, and when the opposition of the quarry owners put an end to this, the enterprising Company substituted road coaches, which ran from August 1879 until, on 18 June 1883, they at last obtained authority to operate passenger services. Meanwhile, relaying had proceeded, and by February 1879 enough had been completed for the locomotives to begin working freight trains between Machynlleth and Corris.

On 4 July, just over a fortnight after the passing of the Act, locomotive hauled passenger trains began to run as far as Corris and four years later, after steel rails had been laid above Corris and space beside the track increased by building retaining walls, the service was extended to Aberllefenni on 25 August 1887, lengthening the run to 6½ miles. Authorised fares were twopence a mile First and Second Class, plus 1½d. if riding in the Company's carriages (how else could they travel?), and a penny a mile Third Class.

To the three principal stations, others at Llwyngwern and Esgairgeiliog were added soon after on the way to Corris, and halts, where trains stopped only when required, at Ffridd Gate (half a mile out of Machynlleth) and Garneddwen (half a mile short of Aberllefenni). In addition, all trains halted at Maespoeth locomotive shed to refill the tanks. Speed was restricted to 15 mph and the journey of 6½ miles took 35 minutes, except in the case of trains having a prolonged stop of five minutes or more at Corris. Before the First World War, however, the Company ran some trains, connecting with services to and from London, which had no booked stop between Machynlleth and Corris, and as these were made up with most of the coaching stock well-filled, those in the Up direction were piloted as far as Maespoeth. Although they cannot be called 'expresses' because they were allowed the normal 25 minutes for the run between the two stations, they must have made a brave sight as they wound their way beside the twisting River Dulas with echoing exhausts and twin plumes of smoke and steam. In the mid-twenties, there were four Up trains and three Down, with another on

---

★ Corris Railway Half Yearly Revenue Accounts 1885 to 1901 (with gaps) preserved in the Public Record Office at Kew (RAIL 1110/88) include a return of the rolling stock owned.

Aberllefenni station on 7 August 1925. The train was standing by the old fashioned two arm signal post.

Saturdays, and other workings between Machynlleth and Corris and back from Aberllefenni to Corris at the end of the day.

The year 1878 during which the locomotives and passenger carriages were delivered and Imperial Tramways bought the railway, saw also the appointment of J.R. Dix, an experienced railwayman from the Cambrian, as Manager, probably also as Locomotive Superintendent, a position he certainly held in 1885, adding that of Civil Engineer in 1902. A very enterprising manager he proved to be; the outwitting of the quarry owners' ban on passenger carrying suggests his adroitness. Well aware of the scenic attractions of the district, he did a great deal between 1878 and 1907 to encourage the development of tourist traffic.

He realised that to achieve this the passenger vehicles would have to be improved. In September 1886, he told the Board that the cars required overhauling and that new ones were needed, but more than a year passed before enquiries made of the Falcon Engine & Car Works resulted in a new car being ordered. This was to be very different from the old ones – a bogie coach, no less, without end platforms but with an entrance in the centre,

Bogie coach as restored and repainted in Corris livery for service on the Talyllyn Railway. The door to the central vestibule was on the far side, and on the near, or 'blind', side was a seat facing across the vestibule. *(Photograph by Colling Turner, 1966.)*

seating twenty-six Third Class passengers and costing £195. It was delivered in August 1888 and 'proved to run very satisfactorily', the Minute Book recording that passengers preferred it to the existing four-wheeled First Class car, so the Board decided to order another. Meantime, however, Dix conceived the idea of commissioning the builders to mount two of the old tramcar bodies on a new frame; this was approved, and when 'the new bogie frame with two old carriage bodies fitted thereon had arrived' from Loughborough in April 1889, it was reported to be such 'a decided success' that it was not necessary to obtain other completely new vehicle. But the cost of conversion, £113 8*s*. 2*d*. including painting and transport, was so much more than had been expected that the Board postponed further reconstruction, until in February 1890 the Loughborough firm, by then the Brush Electrical Co., offered to convert another pair for £87 19*s*. 0*d*., exclusive of transport. This offer was accepted, and on Dix's recommendation, the Board decided 'that the 6 remaining old carriages be fitted upon 3 new bogie frames at the rate of one new frame per year'. By the middle of 1893 the work had been completed and the Corris owned two bogie Composite coaches and four bogie Thirds; but evidently more accommodation was soon needed as another two coaches were obtained in time for the summer services of 1898. It was not difficult to make adjustments to the style of the accommodation between Third Class and Composite, and this was done from time to time.

The conversions followed the pattern of the new coach of 1888: the outer platforms of a pair of tramcars were removed and a central vestibule built on the inner platforms. As stone walls and hedges pressed close in places, platforms and roadside halts were all, like those on the Talyllyn, on the same side of the track, the left-hand side (away from the road) when descending the valley, and the central vestibule through which passengers reached the tramcar seats in the united bodies was therefore fitted with a door on that side only. Painted dark brown and strikingly lined out in yellow, the coaches were generously fenestrated on sides and ends, giving unrivalled opportunity to admire the scenery; but only the small central window in each end could be opened, and these (I noted in 1925) were 'of more value for inter-carriage conversation than ventilation'; so on a warm day with a full load of passengers, as on my journey (which was on a Friday, not a Saturday when a crowded train might have been expected), the atmosphere became unpleasantly stuffy! A wide footboard with a handrail enabled the conductor-guard to pass along the train while in motion and issue tickets to passengers joining at intermediate stops. After more than a quarter of a century, the riding of the coaches was still very good, and the rhythm of the bogies, dér-dér – der-der, was a welcome change from the monotonous tée-dur – tée-der, of the aged Talyllyn four wheelers.

The Corris owned comparatively little freight rolling stock, relying for the slate traffic on private-owner wagons from the various quarries. According to Cozens, there were 150 or more of such wagons about the turn of the century. Those for common slates had slatted or two-plank sides; others were designed to carry slabs which rested against the sloping faces of a triangular trestle mounted longitudinally. The Corris Company's own goods vehicles in the period 1891–1901 totalled eighteen, comprising six large and three small iron-bodied wagons and seven wooden-bodied ones, used to supply the communities with coal, lime, general merchandise and barrels of beer, also two timber trucks and a brake van. More wagons were added later (there were 26 in 1911 and 29 in 1925), one of which was a carriage truck, probably for the conveyance of the road vehicles which the Company by then owned. When timber felling during the First World War created a need for extra timber trucks, these were improvised by fitting a bolster to each of a pair of wagons, some of which were bought from one or other of the quarry companies.

The three locomotives were overhauled and modified at Loughborough during the last decade of the nineteenth century, an entry in the Minute

Book for 11 December 1890 recording that one of them, probably the first to go, was 'about to be repaired at a cost of £105 15s. 0d. plus carriage'. It was more than 'repair' they underwent, for each was converted from an 0-4-0 to an 0-4-2, the rear end being extended and carried on a trailing truck with very small wheels. This enabled the cab to be much improved: hitherto, although the footplate had a roof which was supported on four slender pillars, the front, back and sides had been open to the weather, but now a front spectacle plate was fitted, and then, or maybe later, side sheets and a back spectacle plate as well. The rear end had a very distinctive feature, a large circular hole which could be closed by a disc; through it, the long rods used for cleaning boiler tubes were passed and tubes withdrawn when necessary. The modifications produced a very ungainly-looking machine when seen from astern!

The Corris Railway's involvement in road services for tourists to Tal-y-Llyn Lake appears to have been entirely unpremeditated. In August 1885, the

0-4-2 saddle tank locomotive, one of three built as 0-4-0s by the Falcon Engine & Car Works, Loughborough, in 1878 and rebuilt with trailing truck and sheltered cab by the Brush Electrical Co. in the 1890s. The opening in the rear end is very obvious. The origin of the photograph, which was on sale at an exhibition some years ago, is unknown.

Company made arrangements for a local proprietor to run a coach between Corris station and the lake, which he did for two days but no more: but as the service had been advertised, it was essential to sustain it, so Dix 'procured a conveyance' and ran it at the Company's expense. In the short time from 5 August to the end of the Season, the receipts were £9 2s. 6d., sufficiently encouraging to determine the Board to acquire a vehicle of their own before the opening of the next season. By mid-June 1886, Dix had bought a brake and a set of harness for £20 10s. and had been authorised to spend £30 in the purchase of the first of two horses. Between 1 July and 23 September, this vehicle carried 1,019 passengers and earned £46 15s. 9d. More vehicles were bought subsequently, including a dog-cart for £16 which Dix considered 'would be remunerative in conveying passengers to outlying districts', and also a wagonette. By 1889 earnings had risen to £110 10s. 6d.

The remarkable venture was thus fairly launched, and in 1891 and succeeding years merited a separate entry in the half-yearly accounts. Obviously, the last six months of the year were those that included the period when tourism was at its height, and it was through July, August and September that the Company advertised a regular service by 'Talyllyn waggonettes' (re-designated 'Talyllyn Coaches' two years later), but there were also vehicles available for private hire all the year round, the earnings of which were entered as 'Posting'. Posting brought in £32 13s. 6d. during the first half of 1891 but only £8 13s. 0d. in the second half when the wagonettes were busy earning £96 5s. 3d. – a pattern repeated year by year.

By the summer and autumn of 1896, the horsedrawn vehicles were running between Corris station and the Penybont Hotel at Tal-y-Llyn Lake in connection with one morning and one afternoon train from Machynlleth. The outward drive took 45 minutes, but on return the horses – and often the able-bodied passengers on foot – had to face the steep climb from the lake to the summit of the Upper Corris Pass, so the time allowed was 60 minutes. Passengers who arrived by the morning train and returned by the afternoon one could spend about five hours by the lake, meantime sampling the fare at the hotel. Posters were issued to advertise rail and road services, and a series of picture postcards was produced by a Corris firm for sale to tourists.

The results of this enterprise were very encouraging. During the three years 1895–7 passenger receipts averaged £1,636 14s. 8d., 19.8 per cent of which was contributed by the road operations. Total earnings during the latter period averaged £4,105 9s. 4d. per year, 45.8 per cent of which derived from mineral traffic, 39.9 from passengers, 9.7 from merchandise and 4.6 from parcels, mails and sundries. Revenue continued to rise, averaging £4,273 6s. 8d. in 1899–1901, each category showing an increase, and the road

Corris Railway wagonette at Tal-y-Llyn Lake. *(Photograph: Corris Railway Society.)*

operations providing no less than ten per cent of the total. Meanwhile, in 1893–97 half-yearly dividends between 5½ and 8 per cent had been paid on the share capital of £15,000. But this prosperity was not to last: the demand for Welsh slate had fallen because of competition from imported slates and manufactured tiles; and entries in the Minute Book during some fifteen years before the end of the nineteenth century showed that several quarry companies were in financial difficulty, some unable to meet their debt to the railway company, some closing temporarily and others going into liquidation. The fall in the volume of mineral traffic was, of course, reflected in the dividends: 5 per cent per annum in 1901, 1 per cent in 1905 and thereafter nil.

Much of such prosperity as the Corris achieved clearly owed a great deal to the enterprise of the Manager, J.R. Dix, who not only frequently put forward pertinent suggestions for the Board to consider but often acted on his own responsibility for the good of the Company; and this was recognised in 1888 when his salary was increased to £200 a year. Maybe he sometimes presumed on his position, for there are entries in the Minute Book suggesting that he was growing too big for his boots. Eventually, however, he must have abused his position in some way, for only a very serious misdemeanour could have justified his summary dismissal near the end of August 1907 with a cheque for £50, 'being three months salary in lieu of notice'. His successor, J.J. O'Sullivan, was appointed before the end of the month at a salary of £250 a year.

During the early 1900s, there was discussion of extending the railway itself to Tal-y-Llyn Lake and forming a junction with the Talyllyn Railway at Abergynolwyn. As each had been built to the same gauge, trains would then have been able to run through between Machynlleth and Towyn, two places already linked by the standard gauge coast line, thereby offering an attractive circular tour for visitors. But such an extension would have involved either driving a long tunnel under the Upper Corris Pass, or making the connection by a steep electric tramway running alongside the road. However, since October 1887 the Corris had been managed by the Imperial Tramways Company's associate, the Bristol Tramways & Carriage Company, which presently became extensive builders and operators of motor vehicles, including charabancs, omnibuses and the once-familiar Blue Taxis; and by 1909 O'Sullivan was considering hiring Bristol motor vehicles for the road service to Tal-y-Llyn Lake. As the Corris Company maintained a stud of nineteen horses and the stables at Corris, it was evident that a considerable economy could be made. Moreover, although still considering extension of the railway, O'Sullivan could not have failed to appreciate that a road motor would make the costly extension of rails to Abergynolwyn unnecessary.

No progress seems to have been made before 1911, when O'Sullivan stressed the need, saying in a letter to Bristol that, 'as far as I can see it is the only way of competing with the Motor Charabanc Road Service from Aberystwyth via Machynlleth and Corris and Barmouth to Talyllyn Lake'.★ The result of his plea was that two motor coaches came from Bristol to operate the service from 8 July to 30 September 1911, the hiring charge to be based on the mileage run. They earned £355 10s. 0d., yielding a profit of £57 15s. 8d., and when the same arrangement was adopted in 1912 and 1913, the profit was £36 11s. 0d. and £52 19s. 11d. respectively.

After the 1914–18 war, the number of vehicles increased. In 1926, there

---

★ P.R.O. RAIL 135/2, Letter Copy Book, 15 February 1911.

At Tal-y-Llyn Lake about 1913. At the back on the left is a Corris Railway motor bus. Right of centre is a curious motor vehicle with an awning, and at the extreme right a horse brake. *(Photograph: Corris Railway Society.)*

A well filled Corris Railway charabanc about to set off from Corris station for Tal-y-Llyn Lake. *(Photograph: Corris Railway Society.)*

were seven single deck omnibuses operated on behalf of the railway by the Bristol Tramways & Carriage Company on routes from Machynlleth to Aberdovey and Towyn, to Dinas Mawddwy, to Tal-y-Llyn Lake and Dolgelley (in the summer only), and as far afield as Aberystwyth and Newtown.* The Corris Company itself owned three motor vehicles, two of which were thirty-two seater charabancs and the third a wagonette to carry six; but they also had five horses, and two goods and eight passenger vehicles,† suggesting that a drive in a horsedrawn wagonette was still popular with some tourists visiting Tal-y-Llyn Lake.

By the end of the war, the three locomotives were forty years old and in need of heavy repair, so a new engine was obtained, built in 1920 by Kerr Stuart & Co. of Stoke-on-Trent, and No 3 was sent away for a second reconstruction. The new No 4 was also of the 0-4-2 type, but with smaller driving wheels, 2ft. diameter instead of 2ft. 6ins, and larger trailing wheels 16½in. diameter instead of 11in. As with the older locomotives, boiler pressure was 160 lb. per sq. in. and cylinders 7in. diameter with a stroke of 12in., but the heating surface was less, 109 instead of 170 sq. ft., with the result that the rebuilt No 3 was reputed to steam better. As No 4 was very similar to the 'Tattoo' standard type designed by Kerr Stuart for narrow gauge railways, she was known by that name among the Corris staff, although bearing no visual evidence of it in 1925. After she was purchased by the Talyllyn Railway in 1951, she was named *Edward Thomas*, and the last survivor of the 1878 trio, No 3, accompanied her with the name *Sir Haydn*.

Tattoo had sand boxes, but not so Nos 1 to 3, which therefore carried sand in any convenient receptacle on the front end for use in emergency upon the steep gradients and sharp curves abounding among the trees beside the Dulas, an 'emergency' sometimes obliging the guard to sit on the buffer beam between Machynlleth and Corris, pouring sand from the spout of a large can – almost all narrow gauge and light railways had delicious idiosyncrasies that contributed to their charm!

Originally the railway had no recognised passing loops, as it was worked on the principle of 'one engine in steam', which could when necessary be applied to two engines coupled together. In addition there was a single line train staff for the section between Machynlleth and Corris and, after the extension of passenger services to Aberllefenni in August 1887, a separate staff for that section. As the limitations of the method hampered operations

---

* Information supplied in a letter from the Secretary of the Corris Railway Company to myself, dated 2 February 1926.
† P.R.O. RAIL 1007/45. An undated memorandum, probably prepared for the Great Western Railway in January 1924.

0-4-2 saddle tank locomotive built by Kerr Stuart & Co., Stoke-on-Trent, in 1920. At Aberllefenni on 7 August 1925.

during the busy tourist season, the Board of Trade in 1910 sanctioned the use of 'a Joint Train Staff and Telephone System'.* This not only enabled the pilot engine of a heavy train to return from Corris to Machynlleth while the passengers continued on their way to Aberllefenni, but also made it possible to run relief and special trains as required, the Board of Trade insisting however that trains should pass one another only at Corris.

When the Regulation of Railways Act was passed in 1889, giving the Board of Trade power to order the adoption of Block Signalling and interlocking and the fitting of automatic continuous brakes to all passenger trains, the management of the little Corris Railway was understandably concerned what effect the Act would have on their railway, and late in 1890

* P.R.O. RAIL 135/2. Letter Copy Book, J.J. O'Sullivan to Sir Clifton Robinson, 18 April 1910.

procured an interview with Courtenay Boyle, assistant secretary to the Board with special responsibility for the railway department. He promised exemption from installation of the Block System, but ordered that continuous brakes should be fitted within three years. This was just at the time that one of the locomotives was about to be reconstructed at Loughborough and the tramcars were being remounted in pairs on bogie frames; on Dix's recommendation the Directors decided that the vacuum brake should be fitted to the engine at a cost of £50, to the coaches for £15 each, and to the brake van, which was used on both passenger and freight trains, for £20 (but there is no evidence that the van was in fact ever fitted). But how long was use of the vacuum brake maintained? In August 1925, the coaches still had the fixed metal part of the piping, but there were no flexible connections.

Occasional accidents are chronicled. The Minute Book records one on 17 October 1885, when three coaches and the brake van of the 4.25 p.m. Down train were 'thrown off the line at Machynlleth by a platelayer acting as signalman', whose carelessness led to his dismissal. Cozens notes another on 9 February 1916 during a particularly severe spell of winter weather and after a heavy fall of snow, when the 11.30 a.m. from Machynlleth was partly derailed on a slight curve in Ffridd Wood, the engine being thrown on its side and the leading bogie of the first of the two coaches leaving the rails; fortunately not even the enginemen were hurt.

Unauthorised joy riding plagued the Corris as it did most Welsh narrow gauge railways with their infrequent train services – the temptation to board a wagon and coast down the line was a strong one! But the steep descent from Upper Corris was decidedly risky, as the lad, Joseph Hughes, 'letter carrier', found in June 1886 when he and two children set off in an empty wagon which 'overturned at the Quarry', killing one of the boys and breaking Hughes's leg. The coroner's jury made the unhelpful recommendation 'that wagons should not be left without someone in charge'. Boys, yes perhaps, but one would not expect such irresponsible behaviour from the police; early in June 1886, Dix reported that 'Police Sergeant Roberts had borrowed a wagon at Aberllefenny and travelled down the line to Corris'. The matter was reported to the Chief Constable, but the railway Company was no more ready to prosecute Sergeant Roberts than they were the two quarrymen, who, wishing to join a train the following November, had stopped it by holding up a red pocket handkerchief, thereby rendering themselves liable to two years in prison. The Company preferred to accept their offer to pay £4 4s. 0d. to the Railway Benevolent Institution and £1 1s. 0d. to cover legal expenses. After all, the railwaymen from the manager downwards all lived very close to the ground in a tight little community.

★　　★　　★

GWR Burford Charabanc Car with engine and chassis built by the Bristol Tramways & Carriage Co., and a Buckingham body with canvas hood. At Tal-y-Llyn Lake on 7 August 1925.

On 7 August 1925, the GWR train bore us from Llanuwchllyn to Dolgelley, where the GWR road motor was waiting in the station yard, ready for the run from the Mawddach valley via Cross Foxes to Tal-y-Llyn Lake, and on by Upper Corris to the Dulas valley and Machynlleth. It was an unusual vehicle, though not the only one of its kind in the GWR Company's stud, a Burford Charabanc Car with engine and chassis built by the Bristol Tramways & Carriage Co., and a Buckingham body normally open but protected by a canvas hood and side windows in inclement weather.

Although a leaden sky threatened the rain that came later, the car was open for the first part of the run, but Tal-y-Llyn Lake sat dourly at the foot of a massive Cader Idris whose head and shoulders were shrouded in thick mist, and after a brief halt beside the Penybont Hotel, the hood was raised before climbing over the Upper Corris Pass. As the charabanc car descended the valley of the Afon Deri flowing to the Dulas, quarry workings and inclines became visible on the flanks, and from a terminus beside Upper Corris Post Office, the Corris Railway branch line ran parallel to the road. As this branch was traversed neither by passenger trains nor locomotives, and the wagons were horse-drawn as of old, the light rails originally laid still remained in place. It was joined by private tramways from four quarries, Braichgoch, Gaewern, Abercorris and Abercwmmeiddaw, which about the turn of the century employed between them some 500 men and sent nine or ten thousand tons of slate away by rail annually. Braichgoch, the most productive of them, had well equipped sawing, planing and dressing sheds on the east side of the Corris line, but its workings were in the west face of the valley on different levels and entered by tunnels. One of these passed beneath the Corris branch; the other, higher in the mountainside, was approached by an incline and a bridge over the Corris track. Cozens states that there were four underground levels, and that the original plans for the quarry were drawn up in 1881 by C.E. Spooner of the Festiniog Railway.

The rain was not heavy, so I quitted the GWR vehicle near Corris village and walked up the valley of the Dulas to Aberllefenni, which in 1925 seemed an outpost of civilisation, for it was there that road and public railway ended. From the limit of locomotive working just beyond the station, the old-type rails ran on, laid for a short distance beside the village street which soon deteriorated into a rough roadway giving access to the cart tracks and bridle paths serving the hill farms and cottages scattered up the valleys of two converging mountain streams. The tramway forked, sending a branch up each; one track kept to the bottom of the valley, sending off a loop to a large slate processing shed before swinging north-westward towards the Aberllefenni quarries; but the other, nearly two miles long, climbed the flank and swung from left to right, crossing valley, stream and tramway by embankment and bridges, before heading north-eastward for the Cymerau and Ratgoed Quarries, the latter served by its private tramway with inclines rising some 500ft. from the end of the Corris track. On both branches, as also between Maespoeth and Upper Corris, the pointwork was of the very primitive type with a single pivoted tongue set either way by a kick from a quarryman's boot.

Aberllefenni station, perched on a ledge above the road, had a low platform and a substantial slatestone building housing booking office and waiting room. The Kerr Stuart engine arrived with empty wagons and, having disposed of those, took her place at the head of four passenger coaches. A lattice signal post of outmoded design bore two opposed semaphore arms purporting to give permission to enter or leave the platform, but although semaphores were also in position at Corris, Maespoeth Junction and Machynlleth, as well as at some level crossings, few, if any, were then being used. At Machynlleth, Maespoeth and Corris, the signals, together with the points they protected, had been controlled by levers in a ground frame within a small cabin, but at Aberllefenni the frame

Aberllefenni slate dressing shed, 7 August 1925. The primitive point with a single moveable tongue is clearly visible.

Aberllefenni slate dressing shed photographed on 6 September 1949 by S.H.P. Higgins.

The Kerr Stuart locomotive, Corris Railway No 4, arriving at Aberllefenni with empty wagons on 7 August 1925.

was in the open on the platform; even so, as can be seen from my photograph, the points at the entry to the running-round loop, probably too far off for convenient working from the frame, were controlled by a weighted lever set by hand.

Soon we were away and running down the valley, passing cottages here and there beside the road, and stone-walled fields dotted with boulders fallen from the mountains. At Garneddwen, one of the conditional stops, there was a shelter for waiting passengers and a gated level crossing. The valley of the Dulas is more open above Corris than below, and curves and gradients were therefore less severe, with few banks steeper than 1 in 100. There were cuttings where considerable lengths of stone retaining wall had been built to increase the width before passenger services could be extended from Corris to Aberllefenni in 1887: even so there was little space to spare on either side of the coaches. Approaching Corris, the track ran very close to rows of houses and crossed a road protected by gates, where, it is said, barrels of beer were off-loaded from Up trains and rolled to the entrance of The Slater's Arms! A masonry bridge carried the line over the Afon Deri flowing from Upper Corris, a loop branched off to by-pass the station, and alongside the

Maespoeth Junction, showing signal cabin, locomotive shed and carriage shed. The main line to Corris is on the right. The branch to Upper Corris (horse power only!) climbed up behind the signal cabin. *(Photograph: Corris Railway Society.)*

Ffridd Wood: road on the right, Afon Dulas below the trees on the left. *(Photograph: Corris Railway Society.)*

street was a siding where slate brought by road from neighbouring quarries could be transhipped to rail. The threshold of the station had once been the starting point for the wagonettes and coaches to Tal-y-Llyn Lake, and beside the stable partly dismantled horse-coach bodies lay forlornly, displaced by the blue Bristol motor buses, two or three of which stood waiting.

Corris had been the Company's headquarters until 1907, and the station building, remarkably imposing for so small a railway, therefore housed offices for the General Manager, Secretary and Stationmaster, in addition to waiting room and booking office, all bordering the low platform. Alongside was a similar shed with two tracks to hold four carriages, and the two buildings were covered by gabled timber-framed roofs supported by high slatestone walls. The exits from the shed and the avoiding line were properly protected by catch points set from the ground frame in the signal box.

Presently the branch from the quarries in the Deri valley appeared high on the right, gradually descending to the level of the main line at Maespoeth Junction, where the train stopped beside the engine shed for tank and bunker to be replenished. Controlling the junction and the exit from the sidings was a small lean-to cabin backed by the retaining wall supporting the incoming branch line.

Below Maespoeth the mountains begin to close in, and the train entered on the most beautiful part of its journey, where road and railway, closely confined in the narrow valley bottom, wound their way beside the twisting course of the river hemmed in by wooded flanks. Severe curves and steep gradients of 1 in 70 and 1 in 50 were common, the most testing at Pont Evans where a bank of 1 in 32 and the sharpest curve of all was made more hazardous by grass and fallen leaves which caused engine wheels to slip and unpiloted trains to stall. Beyond Escairgeiliog's modest station, a tramway converged from slate works and the forest in the Glesyrch valley whence the Corris Railway had hauled the timber felled during the 1914–18 war. There followed a very picturesque reach where the trees almost met overhead and the river was glimpsed prettily between the boles. Approaching Llwyng-wern station, there was another branch coming across the river from slate works. Ffridd Gate was a conditional stop, but hereabouts halts were occasionally made at two other points for the convenience of local residents.

Ffridd Gate is indeed an entrance, the portal between the narrow cwm of the Afon Dulas and the open valley of the River Dovey, which the rails presently crossed to reach Machynlleth. The original bridge had been a timber trestle, but over the years the timbers had decayed and in 1906 the directors decided to replace them with steel girders. Erection of four spans with a total length of 203ft. was undertaken by the Company's own staff under the supervision of the Managing Director, Sir Clifton Robinson.

Machynlleth station was alongside the Cambrian Railway's but at a lower level. In June 1903, the directors had authorised rebuilding of the original station on a more substantial scale, to include waiting rooms, stationmaster's office, and an office to which the manager removed from Corris; but the secretary's office had ceased to be local in November 1892 when the then secretary had resigned, 'as arranged with the Directors of the owning Company, the Imperial Tramways Company', whereafter the registered office of the railway had been at Clare Street House, Bristol, the headquarters of the Imperial company.*

The Machynlleth terminus had a running-round loop, another loop where wagons stood awaiting transhipment of freight to or from the standard gauge, and a small and ugly carriage shed of timber and corrugated iron.

Here ended my delightful journey, and I returned by the GWR train via Barmouth Junction to Llanuwchllyn, whither my father, remaining in the charabanc car when I alighted, had preceded me. For me, however, it had been well worthwhile to brave the intermittent rain and ride the Corris.

★ ★ ★

The charm of the little railway, threading its way among the trees in intimate association with the river, no doubt appealed to many, but in vain when motor buses with less unyielding seats and the right to run at twice the train's restricted speed, plyed to and fro upon the road alongside, stopping to pick up passengers or set them down at frequent intervals.

For many years the takings of their own road services helped to fill the Corris Railway's coffers; even the horsedrawn vehicles were earning 24.5 per cent of the total passenger revenue around 1900, and as the motors of 1911 had increased this to 38 per cent, the proportion contributed by the greatly augmented services of the 1920s must have been very considerable.

After the four great railway companies obtained power in 1928 to invest in omnibus companies, in the expectation, largely unrealised, of co-ordinating passenger transport by rail and road and operating services radiating from railway stations, the Great Western took advantage of an opportunity offered them in February 1929 to acquire 53 per cent of the voting capital in the Bristol Tramways & Carriage Co. As part of the agreement, the Corris Railway was to be transferred, once Parliamentary authority had been gained, to the GWR, and the Bristol company's road services outside the City, which of course included those centred on Corris and Machynlleth,

---

* P.R.O. RAIL 135/1. Minute Book, 23 November 1892.

Machynlleth on 7 August 1925, No 4 running round after bringing the train from Aberllefenni.

were to be sold to other operators. The Corris Company's capital, long unaltered, of £15,000 in shares and £5,000 in debenture stock, was acquired by the GWR for £1,000. There was also a considerable debt of £15,844 7s. 4d. owed to the Imperial Tramways Co., presumably because Corris expenditure had exceeded receipts for some years (as it certainly had in 1921), but Imperial agreed to forgo their claim to this, transferring all rights in the debt to the GWR 'in consideration of the sum of One Pound'.★ So by Act of 4 August 1930 control of the little railway passed from Bristol to Paddington.

Deprived of the earnings of its road services, Corris Railway passenger carrying was no longer viable, and on 1 January 1931 the GWR ceased to run passenger trains over it. There may be regrets, but there cannot be surprise; the wonder is that the line remained open for the carriage of freight, including the much diminished output of the slate quarries, for another seventeen years – until, indeed, the River Dovey in spate eroded the embankment by the bridge. The last train ran on 20 August 1948.

★ P.R.O. RAIL 253/673 and 1007/475. The sum actually paid in acquisition of the shares was £808 6s. 5d., but why £191 13s. 7d. was deducted from the £1,000 originally agreed is not clear from the file. Some of the shares were to be registered in the names of nominees so that it should not be immediately apparent that the GWR held more than 50 per cent of the voting capital.

CHAPTER SIX

THE GLYN VALLEY TRAMWAY

So far, three visits to Welsh narrow gauge railways had each been marred by rain. For the fourth, I waited several days in the hope of better weather, but as Friday 14 August was our last day at Llanuwchllyn, my visit to the Glyn Valley Tramway had to be then or never. By this time, my father had had enough of little trains in the rain, so, armed with a sandwich lunch, I went alone. As it turned out, the day was dry and hot, though not until late afternoon did the sun break through cloud.

The GWR line from Llanuwchllyn followed the River Dee closely by a beautiful route, beside Bala Lake, through the gorge to Llangollen and out into the Vale of Llangollen beyond, before climbing sharply away to join the Shrewsbury–Chester main line at Ruabon, from where another GWR train bore me to Chirk. Chirk stands high on the north side of the valley of the River Ceiriog. In 1793 Telford brought the Holyhead Road (A5) from the south down Chirk Bank to the river, across it by a single arch, and up the steep slope to the village by a dog-legged course. But only three years later he began work on the aqueduct which carries the Ellesmere Canal seventy feet above the Ceiriog and, later still, in 1847–8, other engineers took the railway across by a viaduct at a height of a hundred feet. It was from the 'glyn' or valley of the Ceiriog that the Glyn Valley Tramway took its name.

The tramway was promoted to serve slate quarries which had been worked on a small scale since early in the sixteenth century, but there were also lime kilns in the valley, burning coal mined at Chirk, and there were untapped sources of chinastone, silica and granite. A turnpike road served the lime works at Bron-y-Garth, but slate from the quarries around Glynceiriog had to be carried four miles by pack-horses before reaching that road. For the Cambrian Slate Company, formed in 1857 to develop the quarrying, this was wholly unsatisfactory and, by offering to contribute liberally to the cost, they persuaded the Turnpike Trustees to extend the road up the valley, and as a tramway offered an even better means of transport, they made their contribution contingent upon the Trustees' agreement that a private tramway should be laid alongside to the point where it would diverge from the road to reach the GWR and the Ellesmere Canal.

This plan was opposed by the influential local landowner, Colonel Myddelton-Biddulph of Chirk Castle, who insisted that the tramway should be a public one and also serve Chirk village, to which in addition the Trustees should make a road branching from the turnpike. The upshot was that, although the road building was authorised by an Act of 1860, the Bill introduced the following year to enable the slate company to add their tramway was rejected, the Commons Committee stating that an application 'to unite rail roads and turnpike roads' was unprecedented.

There were then two costly schemes for standard gauge branch lines up the valley, neither of which attracted investors, although the second was authorised by Parliament in 1866 at a time of feverish railway speculation. These were followed by a modest proposal for a narrow gauge tramway eight miles long, following the floor of the valley for 5½ miles from Glynceiriog to Pontfaen, whence it would climb the flank and lead to transhipment sidings alongside the GWR at Preesgweene (about a mile south of Chirk) and a wharf beside the Ellesmere Canal, by then part of the Shropshire Union Canal system leased by the London & North Western Railway.

Meantime, a public Bill was introduced in Parliament to aid the promotion of urban street tramways and this, of necessity, conceded the principle that a line of rails might follow a public road. But instead of waiting for this Tramway Act to receive the Royal Assent, which it did on 9 August 1870, the promoters of the Ceiriog line introduced a private Bill of their own, incorporating the Glyn Valley Tramway and authorising the Company to lay rails beside the turnpike road in the valley, for which the Trustees would be paid a rent of £150 per annum. As this received the Royal Assent on 10 August 1870, it is obvious that both Bills had been before Parliament concurrently and that the GVT Bill could not therefore rely on the provisions of the general Tramway Act. This evidently set the Parliamentary draftsmen a problem, for they first stated categorically in the GVT Act that 'No part of the Tramway Act 1870, shall apply to this Act', and then repeated all the sections that did apply!

Although the proposed capital was no more than £25,000, there was marked reluctance to provide even that. The Cambrian Slate Company had lost interest; local landowners supported the idea in principle but not by subscription. So the estimates were cut back, the amount reduced to £10,000, and an approach made to the Shropshire Union Railways & Canal Company, which agreed to subscribe £5,000 on condition that it would be able to ensure that the tramway was properly constructed and afterwards work it. Colonel Myddelton-Biddulph and two other leading landowners then lent their support, and together with G.R. Jebb, the Shropshire Company's engineer, were among those appointed as directors in March 1872.

Enter the Dennis family, whose association with the GVT remained close from its inception to its demise. Henry Dennis had been a surveyor in the service of the Cornwall Railway before moving to Wales. He built a tramway from quarries to the Ellesmere Canal near Llangollen, and then went into partnership with his brother-in-law as surveyors and mining engineers at Ruabon. He surveyed the route of the GVT, chose its peculiar gauge of 2ft. 4¼in., half the standard gauge, and became its engineer.

So after fifteen contentious years, the valley and its slate quarry were at last to have a railway. But those two great viaducts striding across the valley seventy and a hundred feet above the River Ceiriog were reminders that, although laden wagons would be able to descend an incline from the quarry to Glynceiriog and run by gravity down the valley, they would have to be hauled up a steep slope before their contents could be sent away by the GWR or the canal.

By the end of March 1873 the tramway was ready. As far as Pontfaen the track ran alongside the turnpike road, but from there it followed its own right of way, climbing the valley side by gradients between 1 in 22 and 1 in 30 to the crest, where a level stretch preceded an easy downward slope leading to a junction from which one branch led to the railway sidings and the other to a canal wharf.

Assuming responsibility for operation, the canal company found that it had a track but no equipment with which to work it, so it had to supply wagons, horses, stables, warehouse, offices and accommodation for employees, as well as complete the double track incline from the quarry. The revised capital of £10,000 was quite inadequate for all this, and by the end of 1874 had been exceeded by £1,751.

Glynceiriog residents were of course delighted to see a public tramway in their midst and soon asked for a passenger service to be provided. It is recorded that a horse-drawn 'passenger car' began to run on 1 April 1874, but as a 'suitable open car' had only just been ordered from the Ashbury Railway Carriage & Wagon Company of Manchester, one wonders what those first passengers had ridden in – probably a slate wagon with some benches. Certainly wagons were used on 19 December when, as no horse or carriage was available, four passengers travelled down by gravity supposedly under the control of a brakesman – but he was a drunken brakesman and let the wagons gather speed. The party reached Pontfaen intact, but on the sharp curve approaching the bridge over the river the wagons were derailed and the passengers flung into the chilly water and badly hurt. The Board of Trade's Inspecting Officer pointed out that the accident would not have occurred if the regulation that passenger carrying vehicles should 'be moved by animal power only' had been observed.

As is the way with country roads, there were other sharp turns, notably over bridges at Dolywern and Glynceiriog, but the risk of accident was slight, and once proper vehicles had been delivered, so many local inhabitants were eager to travel that two cars were sometimes needed. These covered the 5½ miles from Glynceiriog to Pontfaen in an hour, and David Llewellyn Davies in his monograph records the picturesque detail that the 'driver announced his arrival at each setting-down point by blowing a horn in true coaching style'.★

As long as the tramway was worked by horses (by the autumn of 1875 there were eight horses and about a hundred wagons), Pontfaen was a busy site. The passenger service ran no further, so travellers bound for Chirk had an uphill walk of three-quarters of a mile. Mineral trains, having run down by gravity with a guard, and a horse riding in a vehicle at the back, were divided into short rakes which the horse could haul to the summit of the slope, where the train was reassembled for the descent. Hence, Pontfaen was equipped with a stable for four horses, a weighing machine and a small office.

Had it been possible to raise more capital in the first place, the summit could have been lowered and the gradient from Pontfaen eased but, as sometimes happened even when much more important railways were built, the need to cut the cost of construction greatly increased that of operation. In 1874, the first full year, expenses exceeded receipts by £466 and as the losses continued it became evident that horse haulage over the existing gradients was wholly uneconomic, and when the canal company found that only about a third of the inward and outward traffic on the tramway was canal borne it became dissatisfied. Tramway shareholders were also dissatisfied, believing that the canal company was hindering the exchange of traffic with the GWR.

However, a new source of potentially valuable traffic had been found at Hendre, above Glynceiriog, where a quarry had been opened by the Ceiriog

★ Davies, D.L., *The Glyn Valley Tramway*, Oakwood Press 1962, p. 13.

Granite Company in 1875 and granite setts were made – those stone blocks much in demand as paving, especially where there were urban street tramways and railway yards shunted by horses. Clearly, the GVT had to be extended to that point; equally clearly, if it was to pay its way it had to be worked by locomotives, but although a GVT Act of 1878 sanctioned the extension to Hendre and the construction of a bridge for the tramway at Dolywern, it did not agree to the use of engines because of the steep gradients beyond Pontfaen. There was, however, relief from the annual rent payable to the Turnpike Trustees, who agreed to accept a final payment of £1,000 instead.

Although the canal company took heart from the prospect of increasing traffic from the granite quarry, the tramway shareholders insisted on a change of management, and eventually agreement was reached that the Ceiriog Granite Company would operate the line for an experimental period, purchasing the equipment for £2,000, less than half of what it had cost the canal company. This proved a sound move, and as Colonel Biddulph and Henry Dennis held shares in both the granite company and the tramway, the two concerns became closely linked for some years. The tramway even showed a small profit in 1882, despite liquidation of the Cambrian Slate Company and the consequent loss of the slate traffic. But this happy state did not last, and the granite firm became as dissatisfied as the canal company had been, especially as the statutory powers to extend the line to the quarry and build the diversion at Dolywern had not yet been used.

Clearly, the directors of the GVT would have to assume management and themselves see to the tramway being adapted for locomotive operation. First, the track needed improvement, for derailments were frequent and often gave rise to substantial claims for personal injury and damage to goods. Secondly, an entirely new route had to be found for a track from Pontfaen to the GWR station at Chirk and the canal nearby. Power to build this was granted by yet another Act in 1885, which, after referring once again to the Hendre extension and the Dolywern deviation, sanctioned another by-pass with a bridge at Glynceiriog and, most important of all, agreed to the use of locomotives once the new line to Chirk had been completed; but the rails from Pontfaen to Preesgweene were to be left in place for the use of two small collieries.

In settling the affairs of the unprofitable horse tramway and establishing those of the steam one, existing shareholders were induced to accept new shares at a little less than half the value of the old ones, and £15,000 of fresh capital was raised by the issue of Preference Shares. Of this, £2,641 went in purchasing the equipment the Ceiriog Granite Company had acquired from the Shropshire Union Canal. But there was growing evidence of the lack of firm and effective direction. Creditors of the horse tramway, whose outstanding amounts ought to have been cleared at an early stage, had received nothing by the end of 1887, and though the canal company had agreed to accept £2,400 in liquidation of the £6,000 they had invested, this was not paid until 1888, and then privately by the tramway company's secretary. The price of land needed for the extension to Hendre, instead of being settled amicably, was allowed to go to arbitration, with the result that the landowners were awarded a sum more than three times that allowed for in the estimates. There were peculiar transactions involving directors, who were in dispute among themselves and resorting to litigation. And where some of the money raised by the new issue had gone could not be properly explained.

Fortunately, by 1890 the Company had acquired an able Chairman, Sir Theodore Martin, a solicitor who had developed a large and lucrative practice as a Parliamentary Agent concerned with the passage of railway and other Bills, including the early proposals for the Ceiriog valley. He was also a scholarly author whose reputation led to his being invited by Queen Victoria to write the official life of the Prince Consort, the completion of which in 1880 earned him his knighthood. Living near Llangollen, he had become a director of the Glyn Valley Tramway Company as incorporated by the Act of 1885. Distinguished and influential, he was the very man to take the Chair and restore some order to the chaos of the Company's finances.

It was a daunting task, for by then the little tramway was saddled with a capital structure of £15,616 in Ordinary Stock and £26,377 in Preference Shares, Debentures and Loans – a total of £41,993. As W.J.K. Davies states,[*] the Glyn Valley Tramway, only 8 miles 63 chains in length and with no considerable engineering works, was 'hopelessly over-capitalised'. Even that amount, however, was considerably less than the total expenditure: figures quoted by authorities differ slightly but approach £64,000, representing a cost per mile of about £7,300, compared with £1,814 for the Corris, £2,150 for the Talyllyn, and £10,750 for the Festiniog (with its substantial track and outstanding engineering), each of which owned its own right of way as the GVT in the main did not. Although the earnings of the tramway exceeded the operating costs except in 1921 and 1932–4, the balance was never enough to pay a dividend on the Ordinary Shares, and at closure in 1935 nearly £10,000 was owed in various debts and interest on debentures and loans.

It had been a sorry story. Nevertheless, the tramway served the valley well for fifty years and more, essential to its industries, a boon to its

---

[*] Davies, W.J.K., *Light Railways, their rise and decline*, London, Ian Allan 1964, p. 51.

community, and a delight to those tourists whom it carried up the beautiful valley of the Ceiriog.

Soon after the passing of the 1885 Act, work began on the extensions to Chirk station at one end and Hendre Quarry at the other, as well as the deviations at Dolywern and Glynceiriog, and the replacement of the old 22 or 25 lb. rails by 50 lb. ones spiked to timber sleepers, fish-plated and well ballasted with granite chippings.

While the conversion was under way, the freight and mineral traffic was somehow maintained, but it was obviously impossible to continue the passenger services, and these were temporarily suspended from 31 March 1886. Two locomotives, costing £1,150 each, were ordered from Beyer Peacock & Co. of Gorton, Manchester, a firm with considerable experience in building steam tram engines. Meantime, two engines for the contractor's use were hired from the Snailbeach District Railways in Shropshire, of which Henry Dennis was a director and engineer. That little railway, 3¼ miles long, served lead mines and, hit by loss of traffic because of a fall in the price of lead, was glad to hire out temporarily its two locomotives, *Fernhill* and *Belmont*, 0-6-0 and 0-4-2 tank engines respectively. The 0-6-0 wheel arrangement was far from satisfactory on the sharp curves beside the Ceiriog, and although the Snailbeach gauge was a quarter of an inch *less* than that of the GVT, it was found necessary to widen that of the latter to 2ft. 4½in., which thereafter became the official gauge.

The first of the two new locomotives, named *Sir Theodore* in honour of the Chairman, was delivered in October 1888. *Dennis*, built to the same designs, followed six months later and a third, *Glyn*, with slight modifications, in May 1892. All three were of the 0-4-2 tank type and conformed, as *Fernhill* and *Belmont* did not, to the stringent conditions imposed by the Board of Trade on the design of steam tram engines in those days of the ubiquitous horse and enshrined in the GVT Act of 1885: machinery and fire were to be concealed from view; noise from the blast pipe and clattering machinery was to be eliminated; there had to be a 'suitable fender to push aside obstructions' and 'a special bell, whistle or other apparatus' to give warning of approach. As the speed limit was 8 mph, an indicator was to be fitted and a device to apply a brake automatically if it reached 10 mph. The driver's seat was to be in the front of the locomotive so that he could have a clear view of the road ahead.

The cladding did not go as far as on the Great Eastern's Wisbech & Upwell Tramway where the locomotives were totally enclosed in a box-like structure, but the side tanks hid the boiler, and a metal skirt, with hinged plates for access to the motion, reached to within four inches of the rails. Coke was burnt instead of coal and condensers fitted so that no smoke or

Sir Theodore, built Beyer Peacock 1888, posed at Chirk with a train including two of the carriages with open sides for tourists to enjoy the scenery. From one of two postcards on sale in Chirk twenty years after the last passenger train had run. *(Published by T.E. Hughes from photographs by W. Burns.)*

Glyn (Beyer Peacock 1892) at Glynceiriog. *(Photograph: Locomotive Publishing Company.)*

steam should be visible from the exhaust. A bell mounted on the cab roof supplemented the normal steam whistle. The driver's clear view ahead was ensured by fitting two large windows in the cab back-plate and running with the rear end leading, which had the advantage that the carrying wheels led round the curves. Turntables were provided at Chirk and Glynceiriog.

The driving wheels were 2ft. 6in. diameter, carrying wheels 21in., cylinders 10½in. with a 16in. stroke. The valve gear was Stephenson link motion, heating surface 261 sq. ft., working pressure 150 lb. per sq. in. and weight in working order 14½ tons. Maybe alterations in heating surface and working pressure resulted from later overhaul by the builders, but in a letter to myself, dated 11 September 1925, E.L. Derry at Chirk gave the heating surface as 271½ sq. ft. (tubes 242½, firebox 29) and the pressure as 140 lb. Very wisely, a jack was carried in addition to the normal tool box, for small wagons were easily derailed. *Glyn* was fitted with an additional sandbox, a frame one foot longer to allow more space for footplate and bunker, and a cab protected by a front-plate with spectacles instead of being cut away on each side. The two earlier engines were subsequently fitted with wooden panels to give their enginemen similar protection from the weather. In course of time, the ban on the emission of smoke and steam was ignored, coal was burnt instead of coke, and the condensing apparatus, which overheated the water in the side tanks, was removed.

Another locomotive was acquired later, one of the many 4-6-0 tank engines built in America during the First World War for use on the network of 60cm. gauge light railways serving the Western Front. As by that date the tram engines were around thirty years old and in need of extensive overhaul (*Sir Theodore*, for example, had been out of use since 1920), the GVT bought one of the final group of Baldwins, delivered in March–April 1917. In January 1921 she was sent to Gorton for Beyer Peacock & Co. to alter the gauge and enclose the cab, previously open at the back, and, as they gave her a copper-capped chimney, her appearance was greatly improved. Painted black lined with red and white, and lettered GVT on the tank sides, she looked very smart even in August 1925, as also did *Sir Theodore*, then recently back after being re-boilered at Gorton: although the tramway was never financially prosperous, it long retained its proper pride.

The Baldwin had Walschaert valve gear, driving wheels 1ft. 11½in. diameter, bogie wheels 16in., heating surface 254½ sq. ft., pressure 178 lb. per sq. in. (given in 1925 as 140 lb.), cylinders 9in. × 12in. weight in working order 14½ tons. The cost, including conversion, was £3,000, covered by a hire-purchase agreement with Beyer Peacock. Of course, in no way did she conform to the regulations of 1885 applying to tram engines,

The 4-6-0 tank engine built by the Baldwin Locomotive Works, Philadelphia, USA, in 1917 for War Department light railways, and bought by the Glyn Valley Tramway in 1921. Converted from 60cm. gauge to 2ft. 4½in. by Beyer Peacock, her looks were transformed by the addition of a copper cap to her chimney. Painted black lined with red and white, and with GVT on her tank sides instead of a name plate, she still looked very smart when I photographed her on 14 August 1925. Compare her with the photographs of Baldwins as built and in wartime service on the Western Front reproduced on pages 135 and 138.

not even in running with the cab leading, for she was too long for the turntables and worked with her front end facing Glynceiriog, but by then no one was concerned with such out-of-date restrictions! Although inferior to the old tram engines in steaming and power, she proved very useful, particularly while *Sir Theodore* was out of action.

Bearing in mind the rapid mass production programme under which she had been built and the conditions under which she had been expected to operate, it is not surprising that she ran less smoothly than British-built narrow gauge locomotives, particularly in reverse. When I rode on her in 1925, I did not remark on rough riding, but then she was running with the bogie leading; anyone making his way towards Chirk on the footplate might have received a definitely unfavourable impression, for in time she did

Sir Theodore leaving Glynceiriog. Among the carriages standing in the siding, the one with the clerestory roof is clearly visible. In the foreground is the turntable on the shed road, on the left the track leading from the foot of the slate quarry inclines, and in the distance can be seen the rails running beside the road to Chirk. *(Second of the postcards published by T.E. Hughes.)*

acquire a reputation for giving her crew a shaking, and for that reason she was confined as far as possible to working the mineral trains. That she did this for fourteen years is no mean tribute to the Baldwin Locomotive Works.

The fourteen four-wheeled passenger carriages were a heterogeneous collection. Even the three supplied by the Midland Railway Carriage & Wagon Co. in 1891 were all different. The first to come, used with one of the old horse tramcars for the re-opening of the passenger service on 16 March 1891, had a clerestory roof above a single compartment with slatted back-to-back seats set longitudinally in the centre, and was entered through a sliding door which was later modified so that the lower half opened on hinges and the glazed upper half slid – an arrangement which must have foxed some occupants! The second one was also a type of saloon, but with seats along sides and ends, while the third one, roofed but with open sides, resembled a primitive tramcar as the wooden seats ran lengthways and were reached from end platforms.

Six open carriages for tourists, divided into two compartments by transverse seats, arrived in 1893 at a cost of £60 each; if originally roofless,

GVT four-wheeled carriage as restored and running on the Talyllyn Railway. *(Photograph by Colling Turner, 1966.)*

which seems unlikely considering the uncertainty of the weather in those parts, the defect was soon remedied, and in the early 1900s further protection was provided by boarded end walls. The remaining five were enclosed carriages with two compartments; three of these, delivered in 1893, cost £88 each, plus about £35 for fitting one with upholstered seats for First Class passengers; the other two were added in 1901. All except the open-sided vehicles were lit by oil lamps, whose aroma combined with tobacco smoke and the smell of farm workers' manure-stained clothing to leave an indelible impression on the boyhood memory of David Llewellyn Davies!★ In 1925 the enclosed carriages wore a green livery with buff-coloured panelling above the waist, black lining and GVT in red and gold lettering; earlier there had been elaborate gilt lining and the monogram GVT enclosed in a garter. Two derelict vehicles, one of them the First Class carriage, were acquired in the 1950s by the Talyllyn Railway whose craftsmen restored them, repainting them in GVT livery and fitting up both for the use of First Class

★ Davies, D.L., *The Glyn Valley Tramway*, Oakwood Press 1962, p. 26.

The Baldwin leaving Glynceiriog with a train of mineral wagons, running in reverse alongside the road to Chirk. 14 August 1925.

passengers. Carriages and locomotives were coupled by a bar passing through a central buffer, but chain and hook were provided for coupling to the freight wagons, as mixed trains were often run.

The company owned a surprising number of freight vehicles, 240 or more, between ten and twelve feet long. Some, two of which were vans, were used to supply the scattered communities with coal, bricks, barrels of beer and general merchandise. Others were for special traffic, such as eight bolster wagons run in pairs or fours for transporting long timbers, forty slate wagons, six tar wagons and two brake vans; but by far the largest number was for granite, more than two hundred of them, most with a capacity of 4 tons and a tare weight of 1 ton 12 cwt, costing about £20 apiece, to which the Ceiriog Granite Co. added another twenty privately owned. That company's traffic was indeed the mainstay of the tramway, reaching a peak of 75,989 tons in 1930, nearly 92 per cent of the total freight carried. The greatest number of passengers was 53,720 in 1919. Figures quoted by D.L. Davies* for 1925 show that of the total revenue of £9,966, nearly 79 per cent derived from the carriage of minerals and only 12 per cent from passenger traffic.

* Davies, D.L., *The Glyn Valley Tramway*, Oakwood Press, p. 60.

Transhipping slates at Chirk on 14 August 1925, the GVT wagons standing on a raised track so that their floors were on the same level as those of the standard gauge vehicles alongside.

Freight was exchanged with the GWR and the Shropshire Union Canal at Chirk, where there was an elaborate layout of transhipment sidings at different levels to the north of the two passenger stations. For incoming goods, the tramway siding was at a lower level than the standard gauge one; and for outgoing slate and granite slabs and blocks, the sidings were so arranged that wagon floors were on the same level. A high level line had tipplers for emptying loads of crushed granite into standard gauge wagons alongside; another high level siding stood alongside the canal and had a chute for transfer of contents to narrow boats; and yet another track lay beside a canal basin. In the same area were a smithy, carpenter's workshop, wagon repair depot, carriage shed, locomotive shed, turntable and office.★

As the line was technically only a tramway, its operation was scarcely more trammelled by regulations than any urban street tramway. There was no compulsion to fit automatic continuous brakes, although it was enjoined that the brakes of passenger carriages should be capable of application from

★ See Davies, W.J.K., *Light Railways, their rise and decline*, London, Ian Allan 1964, p. 32 for a sketch plan of Chirk yard.

the locomotive. This was arranged by fitting, underneath the floors, chains which tightened and applied the carriage brakes when the driver used the steam brake on the engine, but as it was found that some of the sharp curves produced the same effect, the arrangement was eventually abandoned!

There was no signalling, no single line token, no restriction to one engine in steam and no insistence that there must be a certain distance between trains proceeding in the same direction; and as for trains travelling in opposite directions, this was permitted if instructions were given to both drivers that they must cross at Pontfadog, one of them being given the key to unlock the points giving access to the loop – a concession which was of great value when mineral traffic was heavy or extra trains had to be run for tourists. If all this sounds very unorthodox, it must be remembered that urban street tramways were operated in very much the same way, on sight, and at much higher speeds. As for the speed restriction to 8 mph on the GVT, it is clear that, officially or unofficially, this was relaxed: timetables from 1908 onwards★ show that the 50 minutes allowed in 1891 for the journey of 6.2 miles between Chirk and Glynceiriog had been cut to 40 minutes even for freight trains, and to 35 minutes for some passenger trains, the latter an average of nearly 10 mph – a bye-law of 1913 stated explicitly that speed 'must not exceed 10 miles an hour when running on the highway'. There were restrictions to 4 mph through facing points and at two particularly dangerous sites, as well as mandatory halts approaching the three most important of the many unprotected level crossings.

Although operated without the stringent safety regulations imposed by the Board of Trade on railways in general, the Glyn Valley Tramway had few, if any, accidents attributable to their absence. Derailments were not uncommon, but these were caused by fractured wagon axles or inadequate maintenance of track. Regrettably, as on all railways great and small, there were fatal injuries to employees: a guard crushed while trying to secure a heavy timber which had worked loose en route; a driver trapped when his locomotive was hit by a laden lorry at Hendre Quarry. Twice, a car parked incautiously on the track at Pontfadog was struck, once in darkness while the owner was in the pub, once unoccupied beside the church where it was concealed from the driver's view by curvature and trees, but even a small tram engine was so sturdily built that it suffered little damage while inflicting a great deal! There were the elements to contend with: one stormy winter evening, an engine working hard up the climb from Pontfaen was damaged

★ Reproduced in Milner, W.J., *The Glyn Valley Tramway*, Oxford Publishing Co. 1984, pp. 37 (1891), 54 (1913), 55 (1927), 60 (1908).

by a tree brought down in the gale, fouling the right of way and not revealed by the acetylene headlamp until too late; far worse were the ravages of the River Ceiriog in winter spate, serious enough to suspend operation for a week in 1900 while track dangled in the swollen waters near Glynceiriog, bad enough in 1903 to erode vulnerable parts of the river bank, threatening road and railway from Pontfadog to Castle Mill.

Even the GVT was required by its Act to carry Her Majesty's Mails, and this it did from 1889 to 1923. The contract provided an income of £80 which was especially valuable as a subsidy during the winter months. There were four mixed passenger and goods trains each way daily, with an extra one down the valley on Wednesdays and Saturdays for local people making their way to market in Oswestry, and two freight trains, one of which ran to and from Hendre Quarry. Extra trains were run as necessary on Bank Holidays, summer Saturdays and for excursion parties – these carried no freight, but even when all fourteen carriages were used, more accommodation was often needed, and so a tail of wagons, specially scrubbed out and furnished with benches, was added, much to the delight of youngsters! A favourite excursion was by horsedrawn barge from Llangollen, crossing Pontcysyllte aqueduct, transferring to the GVT at Chirk, and completed by walking the 3½ miles from Glynceiriog over the Berwyns to Llangollen. Well aware of the local scenic attractions, the Company extolled the Glyn Valley Hotel (formerly the New Inn) at Glynceiriog, stating that 'Visitors will find good cooking, excellent wines and every comfort, combined with moderate charges', adding that they would have access to private river fishing and that the hotel made an excellent centre from which to visit Liverpool Corporation's reservoir at Lake Vyrnwy, the waterfalls high in the Ceiriog valley, and the splendid castle at Chirk which was then open to visitors two days a week during the summer months.

David Llewellyn Davies, who knew the railway as a boy, included in his book an interesting enumeration of the staff employed to keep this little railway running:* a General Manager-cum-Secretary; two stationmasters, who also acted as clerks at the two passenger terminuses; four drivers, one of whom was the shed foreman, and four firemen; two guards; a shunter at Glynceiriog; four men loading, unloading and transhipping freight in the goods yard at Chirk; a permanent way gang of five, who not only had to maintain the track but also trim the hedges frequently because in many places there was so little clearance that young shoots would otherwise whip into open carriages or windows; two cleaners who worked through the night to keep locomotives and carriages in immaculate condition; and in the

---

* Davies, D.L., *The Glyn Valley Tramway*, pp. 41–2.

Chirk station on 14 August 1925: *Sir Theodore* about to propel wagons to the transhipment sidings. The GWR station on the left is securely fenced off! On the down platform is a typical GWR 'pagoda'-style corrugated iron shelter for waiting passengers.

workshops at Chirk, two blacksmiths who were also experienced fitters able to maintain the engines, and five joiners who would certainly have had plenty of work repairing the hard worn wagons – a staff of thirty-two all told.

On the occasion of my visit, I had time before joining the train to walk up through the park to see the exterior of Chirk Castle. Building of this had been started in the late thirteenth or early in the fourteenth century by Roger Mortimer as a massive fortress, part of Edward I's plan for securing the Welsh border, but after Mortimer's disgrace in 1322 it remained unfinished until after it came into the possession of the Myddelton family in 1595, who completed it, not as a fortress but as a Tudor mansion.

At Chirk station, a neat brick booking office and waiting room stood on a low platform adjoining, but firmly segregated from, that of the GWR. *Sir Theodore* was waiting at the head of a train which included some of the open carriages, and it was one of those I entered, the better to enjoy the view and observe as much as I could of the working of the tramway. After rounding a curve on a slight rise within a considerable cutting, the train began the descent into the valley along the reserved track built after the 1885 Act. Against the backdrop of the park woods, part of the line ran along a ledge secured by a retaining wall beside the far more rapidly descending Chirk–Glynceiriog road. Approaching Pontfaen, speed had to be carefully controlled ready for the mandatory stop short of the dangerous diagonal crossing over which the tramway reached the southern verge of the road, the side nearest the river. Trains called here only by request, for there was no habitation nearby, and the halt, marked by no more than a seat and nameboard in the open, was of use only to passengers not wishing to reach Chirk. There was also a long siding, a remnant of the old horse-worked tramway occasionally used on busy days for two trains to pass each other.

From Pontfaen, almost the entire route was that of a roadside tramway, very picturesque, with the winding river on one side, sometimes so close that it washed the revetted bank below the track, and on the other, the road backed by hanging woods. Castle Mill, although like Pontfaen sporting only a nameboard, was a regular stop, for it served a hamlet and was a popular place for tourists to alight and set off walking. In earlier days, a branch line had led from there to the Bron-y-Garth lime kilns. Pontfadog was a great deal more important; the track ran along the road through the village, and as there was a larger community to be served, a brick waiting room and coal depot were provided. If my memory serves me right, we passed another passenger train in the loop, an 'extra' of some kind not shown in the public timetable. Dolywern was perhaps the most charming site on the route, for here the deviation from the roadside took the line across the Ceiriog by a plate girder bridge, and the station lay on private ground at the back of the garden of the Queen Hotel, the former Queen's Head Inn enlarged in 1908 into a pleasant gabled building patronised by fishermen and tourists (it has since become one of the Cheshire Homes). A siding and coal yard were provided short of where the tramway rejoined the roadside.

And so to Glynceiriog, the hub of the tramway's traffic. The passenger station was similar to that at Chirk, lit by oil lamps but with a larger building on the platform – those platforms at the two terminuses that were really unnecessary as travellers joining at the roadside halts managed quite well up the step below each carriage door. There was a brick locomotive shed (by then derelict), turntable, a coal yard beside the river, and a goods and timber yard with warehouse and crane on the site of the old horse tramway terminus beside the Glyn Valley Hotel. Two steep inclines scarred the hillside, down which came laden wagons from the Cambrian and Wynne

Glynceiriog station with *Sir Theodore* at the head of a train about to leave for Chirk. 14 August 1925.

Slate Quarries, both of which had changed in the 1890s from opencast working to mining. And of course along the mineral line from Hendre came not only granite chippings and tarmac ready for road surfaces, but other minerals also.

I had scant time to look around at Glynceiriog before I had to return. *Sir Theodore* had a load of perhaps a hundred tons or more: four carriages, thirteen loaded wagons and a brake van, a tail well twisted on the curves. 'Beyond Castle Mill', I wrote in 1925, 'the fire of our locomotive was made up vigorously in preparation for the stiff climb beyond Pontfaen – to the great discomfort of those passengers who were endeavouring to enjoy the scenery from the open carriages!' The gradient was three-quarters of a mile long at 1 in 63, and the working timetable enjoined that any train of more than 60 tons had to be divided at Pontfaen; so, although I have no note recording it, *Sir Theodore* must have left half the train to be fetched later. Even so, she 'was throwing out live cinders into the woods around' and having learnt a lesson on the outward journey, 'I kept well inside the carriage'.

At Chirk I got into conversation with the driver of the Baldwin, and this led to a pleasant surprise. I had seen, and photographed, him leaving Glynceiriog with a long train of wagons loaded with granite chippings from Hendre, and he was now about to return with empties. Realising my interest, he offered to take me with him on the footplate, not only to Glynceiriog but also along the mineral extension beyond, but he warned me that if I joined him, I would miss the last train back to Llanuwchllyn via Chirk and Ruabon, and would have to walk 'over the mountain' from Glynceiriog and catch the GWR train at Llangollen. His offer was, of course, irresistible, and indeed a walk of 3½ miles on a fine sunny evening, with the prospect of magnificent views over both valleys from the ridge of the Berwyn Mountains, was a bonus, rather than a hardship. But in my subsequent article for *The Railway Magazine* I was careful not to disclose that I had seen the private line from the footplate!

Whereas the River Ceiriog flows in a west–east direction below Llansant-ffraid Glynceiriog, there is at that point in the valley a sharp elbow turn, so

The Ceiriog Granite Company's stone crushing plant at Hendre, 14 August 1925.

that the Ceiriog approaches the village from the south-west. This was the route followed by the extension to Hendre Quarry, which was two miles long and rose 165ft., mostly at 1 in 62, the gradient favouring a train of laden wagons. The scenery was very different from that in the lower part of the valley, wilder and more spectacular as the tramway threaded its way through a narrowing valley beside a foaming river, within sight of hill farms and valley hamlets, a beautiful setting in spite of the scars left by the extraction of granite, silica and chinastone. Sidings from the GVT served the quarries, several of which had private tramways of their own, and a branch line led to Pandy village, where the River Teirw flowing strongly from the mountains had once turned the wheels of its fulling mill. Three-quarters of a mile beyond was the huge gash of Hendre Quarry, and here we halted at the fan of sidings leading into and out of the granite crushing plant and tarmac depot.

The first quarter of the twentieth century had inevitably seen changes in the management. Sir Theodore Martin died in 1909, and was succeeded in the Chair by Dyke Dennis, whose father Henry Dennis had died in 1906. G.M. Jenkins, Secretary and Manager ever since the passenger service had recommenced with locomotives in 1891, died in 1923. But although the three leading figures from the early days had gone, Albert Wynn ably filled the post of Secretary and Manager and, concerned at the condition of wagons and track, set about improving the standard of maintenance, relaying the rails on new sleepers and giving the wagons regular overhaul and heavy repairs when necessary. By 1932 he had achieved much – but alas! a motor bus service direct to Oswestry, and lorries taking tarmac from Hendre to road-works without transhipment, sounded the knell of the tramway. There had been only one passenger train each way daily for six months before the last ran early in April 1933, and all traffic ceased after Saturday 6 July 1935.

Steam tramways running on, or alongside, public roads were rare in Britain, and no other had such a lovely setting. So the Glyn Valley Tramway was a delight to the connoisseur and, had it lasted long enough, a preservation society would surely have been formed to save it. I spent many weeks at The Hand Hotel in Chirk in 1952 and 1953, when the memory of the tramway was still green, and there were even picture postcards of it on sale in the village shop. Locally, its passing was mourned, for it had character, and the service then given by motor buses was even more infrequent.

The grass verge which had once formed the trackbed beside the valley road was still intact and made a pleasant footpath. Above Glynceiriog, all industrial working had ceased, and ten acres given to the National Trust in

1948 included the last mile of the mineral line to Hendre, which was, and still is, maintained as a delightful public walk beside the river.

CHAPTER SEVEN

WAR DEPARTMENT LIGHT RAILWAYS 1914–1918

O f course I never saw the War Department Light Railways, but because
material passed from them to British narrow gauge railways and
were used by contractors on many a construction site, I have included
some illustrations and information to give an idea of how they came into
being, what they were like, how extensive they were, and what they
achieved; matters liable to be overlooked in these days of motorised military
transport.

Early in the 1914–18 war, the Western Front stabilised from the Belgian
coast to the Swiss frontier, with the fighting at its most intense along the 115
miles from the Channel to the French fortress of Verdun. Between those
points, the long trench lines swayed to and fro, and artillery repeatedly
pounded the area, destroying existing roads and railways and ploughing the
ground into ridges and furrows surrounding giant shell holes, conditions
almost impassable using traditional military field transport even in dry
weather, let alone when rain turned the surface into a sea of mud around
flooded craters. Yet the supplies that had to be brought forward steadily
increased, carried in wagons drawn by horses which struggled through
appalling conditions to reach the point where men and mules had to take
over for the final stage to the front line.

It became clear to many that the flow of material could only be maintained
by laying narrow gauge railways from standard gauge railheads to the
forward areas, on roughly prepared formation with few engineering features
and minimal earthworks, using light track, some of it prefabricated, which
could readily be replaced or moved to new alignments, over which would

run standardised locomotives and rolling stock which could be mass-produced. The German armies were the first to adopt this solution, using the well established continental light railway gauge of 60cm. for which they had material already stockpiled. The French soon followed, and by the middle of 1915 had an extensive network laid to the same gauge.

The British high command, however, was obsessed with the belief that frontal attacks would breach the trench lines and the static war be followed by one of rapid movement, leaving railway communications far behind and useless; and it was a long time before this attitude changed. Some individual units laid crude tramways, sometimes with timber rails, over which trolleys were pushed by hand to the front line; but it was direct experience with light railways in a sector British forces took over from the French early in 1916 that convinced the authorities of their value, and led to the placing of orders for material to be manufactured. Of necessity, the same 60cm. gauge was adopted, and as track became available the Railway Operating Division of the Royal Engineers began to install the first sections of a system which grew to a maximum of some 920 miles on the Western Front. At one stage up to 200,000 tons a week were being moved, principally ammunition, but also trench stores, roadstone, engineering and railway material, in addition to large numbers of troops, sometimes about 200,000 men a week, saving them long and wearying marches from standard gauge railheads.

Light Railway Operating Companies and Light Railway Train Crew

A Baldwin 4-6-0 side tank locomotive on a troop train. *(Lens of Sutton)*.

Companies were formed, manned by experienced railwaymen, some drawn direct from home, others from units in which they had enlisted previously. In the autumn, three very senior officers from English railways were appointed to organize military transport, and under them an effective system of train control, still a rarity at home, was established for the light railways, by which the position and movement of every train, locomotive and wagon, as reported by telephone, was visually displayed on line diagrams at control centres.

Rails, locomotives and rolling stock were ordered from British firms, among them Robert Hudson Limited of Leeds, light railway specialists who were prepared to fulfil orders for complete equipment; but though they made track and rolling stock, they did not themselves build locomotives and sub-contracted this work to Hudswell Clarke & Co. or the Hunslet Engine Co., both also of Leeds. The major British locomotive building firms were already fully engaged in completing existing contracts or making munitions, so orders for military light railway engines had to be placed with firms whose output was normally in small numbers for contractors, industrial plants and narrow gauge railways at home, and whose factories were not capable of rapid mass-production.

Fortunately, Hudswell Clarke already had a design for an 0-6-0 well tank engine marketed by Robert Hudson for use on temporary tracks roughly laid at construction sites and therefore eminently suitable for military needs. A few of these engines had already been supplied, but between the end of May and mid-August 1916, forty-two more were delivered, and another thirty followed between October 1916 and June 1918. Andrew Barclay of Kilmarnock built twenty-five of closely similar type, ordered in August 1916 and delivered during February and March 1917. Hunslet, on the other hand, designed and built a 4-6-0 side tank engine suitable for long hauls, and this proved so successful that a first order for forty-five was placed in March 1916; some of these were delivered in August and the last in April of the following year. In all, 155 were built, including thirty more for the Western Front, delivered by September 1917, and another eighty for service in Italy and the Middle East, most of which, however, were not completed until after the fighting had ended. Between them, the three firms manufactured 257 locomotives.

For the authorities at the War Office, committed late to the use of light railways, neither these numbers nor the time taken to complete the orders met the urgent need, and they turned to the largest firm of locomotive builders in the world, the Baldwin Locomotive Works, Philadelphia, USA. Baldwins had a design for 4-6-0 side tank engines broadly similar to the Hunslets, and their manufacturing capacity was so great that they were prepared to produce these in quantity in addition to work they already had in

0-6-0 well tank engine built for the War Department by Hudswell Clarke & Co., Leeds, 1916–18.
(Lens of Sutton).

4-6-0 side tank locomotive built by the Hunslet Engine Co., Leeds, 1916–18. *(Lens of Sutton).*

One of the 495 4-6-0 side tank engines built by the Baldwin Locomotive Works, Philadelphia, USA, in eight months, 1916–17. *(Lens of Sutton)*.

One of the hundred 2-6-2 side tank engines built by the American Locomotive Corporation, 1916–17. *(Lens of Sutton)*.

hand. The initial order for forty-five, at a price of £1,475 each delivered for shipment from New York, was fulfilled in four months from August 1916. A month later they undertook to complete 350 more by April 1917, subsequently agreeing to increase this order by a hundred, and this they achieved, supplying a total of 495 in eight months. Even so, still more were needed, and ALCO, the American Locomotive Corporation, contracted in October 1916 to supply a hundred, which were ready in from four to seven months. These were of the 2-6-2 side tank type, 'double-enders' which could run equally well in either direction, unlike the Baldwins which were so liable to derailment when running in reverse on poor track that reversing triangles had to be provided at likely points.

As the white plume from steam locomotives betrayed their position to enemy gunners, they were detached well before reaching the railhead, and at a marshalling yard their trains of perhaps half-a-dozen wagons were divided into smaller units to be taken forward by petrol tractors. The best and most numerous of these were the Simplex built by the Motor Rail & Tramcar Company of Bedford, whose Mr Abbott had foreseen the need of a light machine even before the outbreak of war. He designed two types of four-wheeled tractor, one of 20 h.p., the other of 40 h.p., with petrol engines driving through the Dixon-Abbott gearbox, with chains to each axle, which gave three speeds in either direction, so avoiding the usual crawl in reverse gear and the need for turntables. The 40 h.p. variety was provided in an open form, a roofed one with bullet-proof shields, and an armoured one which W.J.K. Davies has described as like 'nothing so much as a small tank on rails'.★ These could be built rapidly, the factory at one time turning out twenty to twenty-five a week. In all, some 580 of the smaller kind and 220 of the larger were constructed, coming into use from the latter part of 1916 onwards. British Westinghouse of Trafford Park, Manchester, de-signed 45 h.p. four-wheeled petrol-electric tractors, of which they built a hundred and Dick Kerr of Preston another hundred. There were also the peculiar Crewe Tractors, 132 of which were made by the London & North Western Railway by mounting Ford Model T cars on an underframe with flanged wheels, so arranged that the vehicle could be converted quickly for use on road or rail.

The Westinghouse petrol-electrics were capable of hauling three laden wagons and were easier to handle and rode the track better than the Dick Kerrs. The load of a large Simplex was normally two, and of a small one, a single wagon. The Crewe Tractors proved ineffective in drawing a load but

---

★ Davies, W.J.K., *Light Railways of the First World War*, Newton Abbot, David & Charles, 1967, p. 157.

useful for inspection purposes or transporting personnel.

Of course, an immense number of wagons had to be provided – by the end of the war the total reached 22,895, of which 14,891 were sent to the Western Front. Besides four-wheeled push-trucks for use on trench tramways, there were side-tipping wagons, hopper wagons, tank wagons for paraffin and lubricating oil, ration wagons capable also of carrying a stretcher, and bogie wagons with fixed or removable sides. But in the autumn of 1916, a standard bogie underframe was designed, 20ft. 6½in. long overall, with a screw-down brake-pillar at each end and an axle load of 3 tons which could be sustained by the heavier 20 lb. per yard rails then being introduced. On this underframe, a great variety of bodies was mounted: open with a capacity of 10 tons, each side formed by two hinged drop doors; flat with detachable stanchions or carrying rectangular water tanks; floors with a central well between the bogies to provide increased space for light but bulky loads; floors specially strengthened to carry 18-pounder field guns; and inspection cars. Some lengthened and widened frames were made for the bodies of ambulance vans taking eight stretcher cases and seating four less seriously wounded men. The most remarkable use was in the construction, early in 1918, of Workshop Trains for the maintenance and repair of light railway locomotives and rolling stock when the advance of the armies carried railheads far ahead of the main repair facilities at base. Each train was made up with six covered vehicles housing tools, machinery, stores, swivelling derricks, water and petrol tanks, office and staff room, and electricity generating sets to supply power and light; to some of these trains were attached extra vehicles to provide sleeping and feeding quarters for the staff.

Several of these Workshop Trains were constructed by the Gloucester Railway Carriage & Wagon Co. which, with Robert Hudson Ltd. and G.R. Turner Ltd., was a major wagon builder for the War Department. But there were then many firms that built wagons for overseas railways, the smaller British railways, and private owners such as coal merchants and colliery owners, and more than ten of these played their part in fulfilling the huge light railway wagon building programme.

When hostilities had ceased, many of the light railways were used for several years in work of reconstruction in the devastated areas, and some afterwards in agriculture, one large system in the Artois sugar-beet growing district actually surviving until 1957. But vast quantities, some of it unused, became available from the War Surplus Disposals Board.

The various makes of locomotive had individual characteristics which suited the needs of different prospective purchasers. The Hunslet 4-6-0 engines, highly regarded by wartime crews because of their reliability and stability on rough track, were best for those with long hauls in mind. Hudswell Clarke 0-6-0s, so basic and ugly that the army nicknamed them 'Pugs', had proved admirable for shunting and short trips. The similar Andrew Barclays had something that endeared them to the Australian Light Railway Operating Company, which insisted on retaining them when moved from one sector of the front to another. All three firms had built with customary British excellence of material and manufacture to give long service. The American tradition was quite different: locomotives, especially those built for military use, were, like Model T Fords, intended for hard, rough usage, early scrapping and replacement; and the Baldwins, whose contribution to the war effort had been invaluable, had a reputation for instability caused by the height at which their side tanks were placed. The double-ended ALCOs were more stable and had the advantage that they did not need to be turned at the end of a trip. The well-named Simplex tractors had proved remarkably reliable and versatile.

As might be expected, almost all the Hunslets found buyers. Many went to the Buenos Aires Great Southern Railway in Argentina, which also took Simplex tractors and bogie wagons for use on narrow gauge agricultural lines, some of the Hunslets lasting as much as fifty years hauling trains of potatoes. Other Hunslets were used in sugar-cane growing areas in Queensland. Barclays appeared on road construction projects. Fifty Baldwins went to the North Western Railway in India. Eleven Baldwins were sold in Britain to industrial and narrow gauge railways: one each to a cement works, the Glyn Valley Tramway and the Welsh Highland Railway, two to the Snailbeach District Railways and six to the Ashover Light Railway; of the eleven, one worked for fifteen years, another for twenty-three. The Artois agricultural system used twenty-five or more Baldwins, seven ALCOs, some Hudswell Clarkes, as well as Barclays, Simplex and petrol-electric tractors. An ALCO of 1917, after spending nearly thirty years on a French steam tramway, was given to the Festiniog Railway in 1967, and, as *Mountaineer*, is still at work. So it is clear enough, that with care and periodic rebuilding, at least some American locomotives lasted far longer than their builders ever anticipated!

As for the tractors, the Simplex 20 and 40 h.p. models were certainly popular. The Festiniog bought one of the 40 h.p. *armoured* ones in 1923, removed much of the armour when fitting a new engine in 1954 and added a cab in 1973. As *Mary Anne*, it worked the first passenger train across The Cob after restoration began. Many others were acquired by contractors; one of the smaller ones was to be seen on railway building at Charlton Kings, Cheltenham, in 1923, one of each during the construction of reservoirs in Colsterdale, Yorkshire, in 1928. Even a Crewe Tractor found a home on the

One of the 580 Simplex 20 h.p. tractors built for the War Department by the Motor Rail & Tramcar Co. of Bedford and delivered from the latter part of 1916 onwards. Seen at work on railway building at Charlton Kings, Cheltenham, 22 April 1923.

Interpretation of a very old photograph of ROD No. 309 in action during World War I. *(Courtesy Hunslet Engine Co.)*

Ravenglass & Eskdale Railway in the early 1920s!

The gauge of some locomotives had to be adjusted or altered to suit their new owners, but the Ashover Light Railway prudently adopted the 60cm. gauge so as to be able to equip the line almost entirely with ex-War Department material as built.

CHAPTER EIGHT

THE ASHOVER LIGHT RAILWAY

My acquaintance with the Ashover Light Railway was limited to what I saw through the window of an LMS train on the Midland line between Chesterfield and Derby on a number of journeys from Leeds or York to Cheltenham in the late 1920s. From a corner seat facing the engine (always my favourite position) on the right-hand side of the compartment, there was a view of Clay Cross Yard, generally with a Baldwin engine at work, before a southbound train plunged into a cutting and tunnel. Two miles further on was Stretton where main line and narrow gauge stations were close together, and I might catch sight of a light railway passenger train waiting to make connections. These scanty sightings were fortunately supplemented by a set of six sepia postcards issued by the Locomotive Publishing Company, which I obtained in 1926.

Built in the 1920s, as also were the Welsh Highland Railway, the Sand Hutton Light Railway and the Romney, Hythe & Dymchurch Railway, the Ashover was one of the last of the long line of light railways designed for public service before road motor competition put a stop to further promotion.

Clay Cross, a small town five miles south of Chesterfield, was then an active centre of coal mining and iron smelting in the hands of the Clay Cross Company, which had been founded in the late 1830s by George Stephenson after valuable seams of coal had been discovered during the driving of Clay Cross Tunnel. Amongst Stephenson's nine colleagues were William Jackson and Edward Betts, partners with Samuel Morton Peto and Thomas Brassey in the leading firm of railway contractors. As the years passed, the number of Clay Cross partners dwindled to three, and in 1871 Sir William Jackson bought out the other two, whereafter the firm, formed into a limited company in 1913, remained in the hands of the Jackson family.

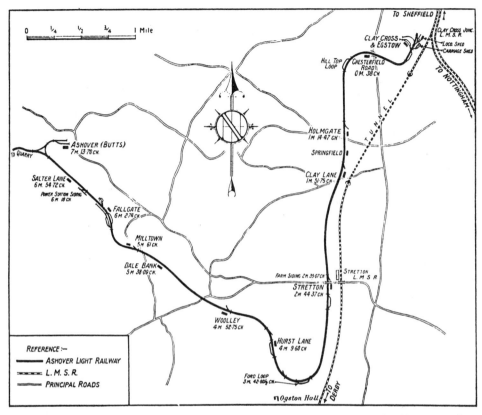

Sketch map showing the V-shaped route of the Ashover Light Railway. *(Reproduced by courtesy of The Railway Magazine.)*

Ashover was the centre of a rural area some three miles to the west of Clay Cross in the valley of the River Amber, which flows into the Derbyshire Derwent and so to the Trent, and in the countryside around were found deposits of limestone, fluorspar, barytes and gritstone, which The Clay Cross Company secured by purchasing, in 1918, the estate in which they lay. Proposals for a railway to link this area with the industrial works and the Midland Railway soon followed.

Although Ashover and Clay Cross are less than 3½ miles apart as the crow flies, any such railway had to follow a V-shaped route to avoid the hills confining the valley of the Amber. It therefore had to run southwards from Clay Cross, following a tributary of the Amber for more than 3½ miles, almost all on a descending gradient, to Ford at the lowest point (in both senses) of the V, before turning to the north-west up the valley of the Amber for almost 3½ miles more to reach Ashover, 152ft. higher. The original intention was to build a standard gauge branch from the Midland at Stretton, and to carry goods and passengers as well as minerals, but although construction was authorised by a Light Railway Order in 1919, the effect of post-war inflation was so great that nothing was done.

Instead, the Clay Cross Company sought the advice of Colonel H.F. Stephens of Tonbridge, engineer and manager of a scatter of light railways, standard and narrow gauge, all operated with stringent economy. Appointed Consulting Engineer, Stephens suggested to Brigadier General G.M. Jackson, the prime mover on behalf of the Clay Cross Company, that the railway should be built to the 60cm. gauge, for which almost all the material, track, locomotives and wagons, could be obtained very cheaply from the War Surplus Disposals Board. The cost of the narrower formation would be less, dependence on Midland Railway tracks between Stretton and Clay Cross avoided, and direct connection made with the existing narrow gauge railways serving the works. As most of the traffic would be minerals to be used by the Company, very little transhipment would be involved.

Choice of a different gauge, and extension from Stretton to Clay Cross, meant that another Light Railway Order had to be obtained, and when the Company applied for this, they clearly intended to build a private line solely for their own use. The Ministry of Transport, however, insisted that the railway should provide a public service for carriage of passengers and general merchandise as well, and on this understanding the Order was issued on 13 November 1922.

General Jackson was then able to go 'shopping'. At a sale of ex-War Department material he offered £1,000 for four Baldwin engines; this was scornfully rejected, but as no other offers were received, the Disposals Board subsequently wrote accepting his offer if it was still open! Fifty open wagons, with timber bodies mounted on wooden or steel underframes carried on bogies, were also bought, for £2,392 8s., and later another twenty from scrap merchants even more cheaply, for £450. One was fitted with a tar tank to service a roadstone plant, and four were sent to the Gloucester Railway Carriage & Wagon Company which used the bogies in building four passenger carriages, costing £1,634, all equipped with vacuum brakes and electric light – steam heating was fitted later. The carriage bodies were of timber with longitudinal seats of tramcar type in two saloons, and had end doors opening to entrance vestibules. Livery was Midland Red, lined out in gold and lettered 'Ashover Light Railway' in full above the windows. Wagons were painted light grey and lettered ALR in large white letters. Locomotives and rolling stock retained the WD centre buffer-couplings.

The Baldwin locomotives retained for some time, and in the early days

4-6-0 side tank locomotive *Peggy*, built by the Baldwin Locomotive Works to the order of the War Department for use on the 60cm. gauge light railways laid on the Western Front and elsewhere during the 1914–18 war. *(Reproduced from a set of six postcards issued by the Locomotive Publishing Company 1925–26.)*

Ashover Light Railway train at Clay Cross, showing *Peggy* at the head of two of the four passenger coaches built by the Gloucester Railway Carriage & Wagon Company, using bogies from WD wagons.

actually used on occasion, the water lifting gear originally fitted for filling the tanks from water-logged shell holes. The austere stove-pipe chimneys had, of course, the lid-like hinged disc typical of foreign engines which spent their idle hours in the open instead of in a shed, but these disappeared when new chimneys with shapely cast iron caps were fitted to improve steaming – improving appearance at the same time.

Their condition varied: all needed some overhauling, but one had been among the first forty-five Baldwins to be delivered (in the closing months of 1916) and would therefore have seen the best part of two years' rough usage on the Western Front; so it is not surprising that after being used during construction of the Ashover line, she was found in need of such heavy repair that replacement was a better proposition. In fact, two more Baldwins were bought in 1925 from the Sheffield scrap merchants, Thomas W. Ward Limited. Reasonably enough, Ward demanded a higher price, £300 each, than the Disposals Board had accepted. The extra engine was sensibly acquired as a source of spare parts, although in course of time the Clay Cross Company's works proved fully capable of making anything required, beginning with back sheets to enclose the WD cabs. In the end, after some years, the story of the steam locomotives became that of W.S. Gilbert's *Yarn of the 'Nancy Bell'*, in which those who escaped from a shipwreck ended up one by one in the cauldron until a sole survivor remained! Here, in Derbyshire, parts were so freely transferred from one engine to another that the last in service probably retained little of its original material except the name plates.

Officially, livery of the locomotives matched that of the coaches, but it is evident that not all the engines were so treated, one or more appearing in unlined black, as did all of them when they became due for repainting – a sad, if inevitable, concession to economic pressures. All were fitted with brass plates and were named by Brigadier General Jackson, the Managing Director, after his sufficiently prolific family: *Hummy*, *Guy*, *Joan*, *Peggy*, *Bridget*, the sixth taking the name plates of *Guy* from the scrapped original. The survivor of these was withdrawn in 1950 bearing the name *Peggy*.

Internal-combustion locomotives were used spasmodically from 1927 onwards, but although Colonel Stephens, who remained as Consulting Engineer until his death in 1931, made considerable use of them and also of petrol railcars on the railways he managed, he evidently failed to influence the Ashover in their favour. The Clay Cross Company bought from the Disposals Board, a number of the WD 40–45 h.p. petrol-electric locomotives built by British Westinghouse and Dick Kerr, but this was primarily to make other use of their electric motors. One was retained as a shunter and to bank heavy trains up the gradient from Ford to Clay Cross, but after performing these and other duties for several years, she was laid aside because her petrol consumption was so heavy, and when returned to service she was confined to shunting. In 1939, discarded parts of others were reassembled and fitted with a more economical diesel engine in order to work stone trains, but a limited speed of 6 mph led to relegation to shunting duties and, finally, to immobilisation as a generator. Not until the Baldwins were thoroughly run down did the railway make better use of an internal combustion locomotive, acquiring in 1948 a new 48 h.p. four-wheeled diesel-mechanical of the Planet type, a development of the Simplex, fitted with a Perkins engine driving through a fluid flywheel, three speed gearbox and chains to the axles. In 1981, long after the Ashover Light Railway had closed, this locomotive passed to the Festiniog Railway.

The route, just under 7¼ miles long, was chosen by Jackson himself, not by Colonel Stephens who claimed to have done no more than give advice on this and other matters.★ Although there were a few steeper lengths in favour of loaded mineral trains, the gradients elsewhere did not exceed 1 in 80 in either direction. Earthworks were light, with cuttings no more than fourteen feet deep, but there was one considerable embankment, 20ft. high, leading to the girder bridge crossing the Sheffield–Chesterfield–Derby main road near Clay Cross. Construction of the line was carried out by the Clay Cross Company itself, using its own employees supplemented by some local labour and a steam navvy, and as the Company's works necessarily had experienced platelayers, these laid the track, for the most part ex-WD rails. Although most sources, including contemporary issues of *The Railway Yearbook*, record the gauge as 2ft., it was in fact just under 23⅝in., the equivalent of 60cm.

The Midland Railway station named Clay Cross was about 1½ miles north-east of the town, close to the important junction between the main lines to Ambergate and Derby on the one hand, and to Leicester and Nottingham on the other. The Derby line passed under the town in a tunnel, and the town goods station and Clay Cross Company's yard were reached by a branch line. The Ashover's station, named Clay Cross & Egstow, was at the junction with the works railways, three-quarters of a mile from the town centre. About the same distance from the town, beside the Chesterfield Road bridge, was another station, rather more useful because of a frequent bus service, which also brought would-be passengers from Chesterfield. Those coming from further afield changed from main line to narrow gauge trains at Stretton. There were, however, three halts at level crossings, each about a quarter of a mile west of Clay Cross, which were

★ According to Plant, K.P., *The Ashover Light Railway*, Oakwood Press, 1965, 1987, p. 23.

The train posed at Clay Cross, with the Clay Cross Company's works – and tall slag heap – in the background on the left. The town is to the right, on the rising ground under which the Midland Railway line to Derby passed in a tunnel.

really the most convenient points for townsfolk to join the Ashover trains.

Gradually, works, slag heaps and the urban area receded into the distance, and rather more than a mile beyond Stretton, the line swung into the beautiful, well timbered valley of the River Amber, which it then followed closely and crossed frequently. There were four halts within the space of two miles before reaching Fallgate, the centre from which most of the minerals were carried to the Clay Cross works; tracks branched off to a limestone quarry with crushing and screening plant and loaded hopper, entered two adits of the fluorspar mines and served their washing plant, led to an electricity generating station burning coal from Clay Cross, and, some years later, also to a tarmac plant.

A little over half a mile from Fallgate was a halt known as 'Salter Lane for Ashover', close to the village and intended to be the passenger terminus until it was realised that the site was too confined. A better one lay half a mile beyond, beside the rails leading to the Company's Butts limestone quarry, so the terminus became Ashover Butts, further from the village but reached by a far better road than the steep Salter Lane. A hundred yards from the station, the Clay Cross Company built a café, named 'Where the Rainbow Ends' after a popular play, and there teas and even late dinners were served during the season.

The uneasy motion of the Baldwins when running in reverse made it

Ashover Butts station. Standing in the goods siding are two ex-WD bogie wagons, one with its drop-side doors open.

The reversing triangle at Ashover Butts. The locomotive has propelled its train from the station (in the distance on the extreme left) preparatory to setting off for Clay Cross along the base of the triangle, which is obscured by re-touching and the branches of the tree in the foreground.

essential to turn them at the end of each trip, but instead of installing turntables and running-round loops, triangles were laid so that the entire passenger train was turned and uncoupling and recoupling avoided. Moreover, by placing the stations at Clay Cross and Ashover Butts on one of the short sides leading to a dead end, the train could stand there without obstructing the movement of wagons along the base of the triangle leading to the works or quarry. Station buildings were of timber, with an open-fronted waiting room between the booking office and a store intended for parcels and small consignments of goods, though little of such traffic was, in fact, ever handled. Halts were provided with a three-sided wooden shelter.

Light railways were not obliged to erect semaphore signals, and the Ashover had none, but safety was ensured by the provision of single line staffs and a telephone circuit. There were four intermediate crossing places, and each of the five sections had its own brass staff and engraved metal 'tickets' in two sets, one for each direction, for use when one train was to be followed by others. There was a fifth loop at Ford, the lowest point on the line, used, not for trains to pass, but for a banking engine to stand while waiting to assist mineral trains up the bank, much of it at 1 in 80, to Clay Cross. Points were worked by weighted levers, the weight ensuring that those controlling entry to a passing loop always returned to the position for the left-hand track. Those leading from sidings to the running line were locked so that they could be thrown over only when released by the correct key carried with the staff; wagons were prevented from fouling the running line by scotch blocks instead of catch points.

That the safeguards were adequate is shown by the record: no one, not even a railway employee, was killed during the twenty-six years of operation. One locomotive was overturned by a runaway lorry, another derailed by an obstruction on the rails; an unobservant motor-cyclist ran into a locomotive at an ungated crossing, but, although badly injured, survived; several times wagons escaped from Butts Quarry and set off down the line, twice ending up by collision or derailment at Fallgate, but on another occasion clearing a short 1 in 80 rise and careering for 3½ miles before coming to rest at Ford, checked by the start of the ascent to Clay Cross. Fortunately, the runaways caused no greater damage than destruction of a set of level crossing gates at one of the only two roads so protected, the many open crossings having no more than cattle-guards on each side.

Passenger traffic, which Brigadier General Jackson had never intended to cater for, developed to a wholly unexpected extent as soon as the railway was opened to the public on 7 April 1925. Ashover and the valley of the Amber were widely known for their beauty, attracting alike those who sought a day out and visitors who appreciated a holiday resort in the peaceful setting of a Derbyshire dale, staying in the hydros, hotels and inns in the village, swelling the population and bringing prosperity during the summer months. Before the light railway was built, these had to come by train to the Midland station at Stretton and thence by road, but now they could reach Ashover more easily and cheaply, especially the day trippers for whom the return fare was one shilling – and they came in thousands; 5,000 during the first Easter weekend, 5,300 at Whitsun, 63,657 by the end of the year.

To carry them, more vehicles were soon needed. Temporarily, two wagons were roughly converted by fitting seats and a canopy; but when the British Empire Exhibition at Wembley closed in 1925, the Ashover took the opportunity to buy eight of the carriages which had been used on the curious Never-Stop Railway, operated by a constantly revolving screw thread between the rails with varying pitch that slowed the vehicles to a very low speed in the stations and accelerated them as they left. The carriages were roofed, but entirely open on the side where passengers boarded or alighted; for use on the Ashover, the bodies were remounted on ex-WD wagon underframes, and, like the temporary ones they replaced, were piped for vacuum but not braked.

It took time to establish the mines and quarries in working order, so for a while mineral traffic was handled by attaching wagons to the passenger trains. Of these, there were six or seven each way daily, with extras on Wednesdays and Saturdays, and four on Sundays. Speed was limited to 15 mph, with restriction to 5 mph at major level crossings and 10 mph at others, so schedules were generous: 49 minutes to Ashover, 55 minutes to Clay Cross (no doubt because the trains might include mineral wagons to be hauled up the bank from Ford); some took four or five minutes less, others up to eight minutes more, depending on the length of the stop at Stretton to connect with LMS trains in one or both directions. But even the quickest trains averaged less than 10 mph overall.

The booming passenger traffic of the first year, earning £1,079, was never approached again, for regular road motor services and day excursions by charabanc from the towns soon proved quicker and more convenient, so that, in spite of the day return fare being reduced first to 9d. and then to 6d., passenger revenue declined steadily. Winter services were withdrawn in 1931; and, after five years during which trains ran on Wednesdays, Saturdays and Sundays in the summer season only, all regular passenger carrying ceased.

However, freight earnings, £1,464 in the first nine months after opening, reached a maximum of £5,072 in 1927, averaged £2,668 over the next ten years, and even £1,559 in 1943–9. But by then the railway had been running at a loss for some years, the Clay Cross Company was receiving its minerals by road, and it was no longer profitable to work Butts Quarry to provide the ballast hitherto supplied to British Railways and carried in narrow gauge wagons for transhipment at Clay Cross.

So the Ashover Light Railway, which had cost some £40,000 to build and equip in 1925, closed on 31 March 1950 after no more than a quarter–century of service.

BIBLIOGRAPHY

Anonymous. *Welsh Mountain Railways*. Paddington, Great Western Railway, 1924.

Behrend, George. *Gone With Regret*, Chapter 9, 'The Last Days of the Corris'. Lambarde Press, Sidcup, Kent, 1964 edition.

Bett, Wingate H., and Gillham, John C . *Great British Tramway Networks*. The Light Railway Transport League, London, 4th edition, 1962.

Boyd, J.I.C. *Narrow Gauge Rails in Mid-Wales*. Oakwood Press, 1952.
   The Festiniog Railway (two volumes). Oakwood Press, 1975 ed.

Cozens, Lewis. *The Corris Railway*, 1942, reprinted by The Corris Railway Society, 1972.

Davies, David L. *The Glyn Valley Tramway*. Oakwood Press, 1962.

Davies, W.J.K. *Light Railways; their rise and decline*. Ian Allan, London, 1964.
   Light Railways of the First World War, A History of Tactical Rail Communications on the British Fronts, 1914–18. David & Charles, Newton Abbot, 1967.

Johnson, Peter. *A Traveller's Guide*. Festiniog Railway Company, Porthmadog, 1983.
   Festiniog 150, The History of the Festiniog Railway. Ian Allan, London, 1986.
   Festiniog Railway Gravity Trains. Festiniog Railway Heritage Group, Leicester, 1986.
   and Weaver, Rodney. *Great Preserved Locomotives, Talyllyn Railway*. Ian Allan Ltd, London, 1987.

Lee, Charles, E. *Narrow Gauge Railways in North Wales*. The Railway Publishing Co, London, 1945.

Lewis, M.J.T. *How Ffestiniog Got its Railway*. Railway & Canal Historical Society, 2nd edition, 1968.

Locomotive Railway Carriage & Wagon Review, Vol 32, August 1926, pp. 246–8, (Corris Railway).

Milner, W.J. *The Glyn Valley Tramway*. Oxford Publishing Co, 1984.

Plant, K.P. *The Ashover Light Railway*. Oakwood Press, revised edition, 1987.

Prideaux, J.C.D.A. *The English Narrow Gauge Railway; A Pictorial History*. David & Charles, Newton Abbot, 1978.

Public Record Office, Kew. Corris Railway Material, RAIL 135/1, 135/2, 253/673, 1007/475, 1110/88.

Railway Magazine, Vol 57, October 1925, pp. 279–84 (Ashover Light Railway); Vol 58, April 1926, pp. 283–6 (Glyn Valley Tramway); Vol 58, June 1926, pp. 431–5 (Talyllyn Railway); Vol 96, September 1950, pp. 579–82 & 594–5 (Ashover Light Railway); Vol 127, February 1981, pp. 62–4 (Talyllyn Railway); Vol 133, August 1987, pp. 490–1 & 524–6 (Festiniog Railway).

Rolt, L.T.C. *Railway Adventure, The Story of the Talyllyn Railway*. David & Charles, Newton Abbot, 1961.

Rolt, L.T.C., edited by. *Talyllyn Century*. David & Charles, Newton Abbot, 1965.

Talyllyn Railway Guide. Recent issue undated.

Taylorson, Keith. *Narrow Gauge at War*. Plateway Press, Croydon, 1987.

White, Christopher. *Talyllyn Railway Extension Abergynolwyn to Nant Gwernol*. The Talyllyn Railway Preservation Society, Tywyn, 1978.

Whitehouse, P.B. *On the Narrow Gauge*. Thomas Nelson & Sons, Edinburgh, 1964.

Winton, John. *The Little Wonder, 150 Years of the Festiniog Railway*. Michael Joseph, London, revised edition, 1986.